Th
Out

A GUIDE TO REACH THE LGBTQ+ COMMUNITY

By Tyeesha Holt

Copyright 2019

Tyeesha Holt Ministries
www.tyeeshaholt.com

No part of this book, aside from the Scriptures quoted from the Holy Bible, may be reproduced by any means without the expressed written permission from the author.

Edited by Victor D. Franco
vdf.boa@gmail.com
www. blazeascension.com

All rights reserved by Tyeesha Holt

Other books by Tyeesha Holt:
- *Nothing Gay About Being Gay*
- *Bunkee Smackers & Kraven Kay God's Image In Full Armor Children's Book*

Content

- **Preface** ... 1
- **The Stonewall Riots: The Root of the Gay Rights Movement** ... 5
- **What is the Practice of Homosexuality?** ... 8
- **The Most Common Developmental Patterns of Homosexuality** ... 9
- **How Living in an Over-Sexualized Culture Can Play a Role in Homosexuality** ... 13
- **How Gender Bias Can Play a Role in Homosexuality** ... 17
- **What is the LGBTQ+ or Gay Agenda?** ... 19
- **The Main LGBTQ+ Symbol** ... 21
- **Unspoken Dangers, Warnings and Lies** ... 23
- **Terms and Definitions** ... 24
- **Gay Pride** ... 30

- What Does the Bible Say About Homosexuality? ... 33

- Understanding the Spiritual Influences Behind Homosexuality ... 44

- Can a Person Be Born Gay? ... 46

- What Does a Person Mean When They Say They Were 'Born Gay'? ... 50

- How to Open Conversation with Someone Who Believes They Were Born Gay ... 53

- Preparing Leaders of the Church ... 56

- What Do I Do if They Want to Lead in the Church? ... 58

- Introduction of Their Homosexuality: Trauma and Choice ... 60

- Introduction of Their Homosexuality: Exposure ... 69

- The Key to Helping Victims of Exposure ... 70

- Why Listening to their Story is Important ... 72

- **Ways to Educate Your Congregation** ... 75

- **Understanding the Cost of One Walking Away From Their Lifestyle** ... 77

- **The Unraveling Process of Healing** ... 78

- **The Importance of Your Kind of Approach** ... 80

- **The Wrong Approach Creates Defense Mechanisms** ... 83

- **Discovering a Better Approach** ... 86

- **What the Way Out *is* and *is Not*** ... 90

- **Key Points of The Way Out Process** ... 92

- **Salvation** ... 95

- **Deliverance** ... 99

- **Renewing the Mind** ... 100

- **Obedience** ... 102

- **Literature and Scripture** ... 103

- ➤ How to Respond When Someone with Same Sex Attractions *is not* Engaged in Same Sex Sexual Activity ... 107

- ➤ How to Respond When Someone *is* Engaged in Same Sex Sexual Activity ... 111

- ➤ Things to Mention to Parents in the Church Who Have Discovered Their Child or Adolescent is Identifying as Gay ... 116

- ➤ Discussion Questions ... 119

- ➤ Things to be Aware of and Look for in the Home After Your Child Comes Out ... 120

- ➤ A General Approach For Dealing With Sexually Confused Children ... 122

- ➤ Frequently Asked Questions From Parents ... 126

- ➤ Did I Really Miss the Signs? ... 130

- ➤ Did I Fail as a Parent? ... 134

- ➤ What Are Good Resources and Bad Resources and How Can We Tell the Difference? ... 137

- ➢ **What if I Have Accepted My Child and Am Now Feeling Convicted Upon Becoming Educated on What Homosexuality Really Is?** ... 138

- ➢ **Parents: General Do's and Don'ts** ... 139

- ➢ **Do I Attend the Gay Wedding of My child or Loved One?** ... 144

- ➢ **How to Treat The Partner of My Child or Loved One** ... 146

- ➢ **Understanding Why People Go Back Into the Homosexual Lifestyle After Years of Being on the Straight and Narrow** ... 148

- ➢ **The Way Out Conclusion** ... 152

Preface

The Way Out is a resource Guide to assist the church with reaching those in the LGBTQ+ community. It also serves to aid those within the body of Christ who struggle with homosexuality or same sex attraction, also known as SSA. If you're a pastor, minister, teacher, leader, or believer who is struggling or has struggled with homosexuality or SSA, this book is also for you. It will help shed light on some of the issues within you have yet to understand or address.

If you're reading this book, it is likely you fall into one of the following categories.

- **You're a parent whose child struggles with sexual identity or SSA**

- **You have a friend or family member who practices homosexuality**

- **You have struggled with SSA or overcome homosexuality in the past**

- **You are currently struggling with homosexuality and searching for ways to overcome**

- **You're a believer who finds it difficult to approach a person practicing homosexuality**

- **You're a church or spiritual leader interested in ministering to someone desiring to overcome SSA or cease practicing homosexuality**

- **You're a pastor looking to make his/her church a friendlier, healthy environment for those struggling with SSA or practicing homosexuality**

If you relate to any of these categories, this Guide contains general information that can be used universally within the body of Christ. It can help you gain an overall understanding of homosexuality or SSA. While this book may not answer *all* of your questions, it addresses some of the most common associated issues. Everything written herein is derived from Scripture, personal experience with homosexuality, and revelation I've received from the Holy Spirit during my journey out of the lifestyle. The Bible states "all Scripture is God-breathed and is useful for teaching, rebuking, correcting and training in righteousness" (*2 Timothy 3:16*). Therefore, I reference Biblical Truths from the complete Word of God to draw conclusions for the concepts presented in this Guide.

I have loaded this Guide with information to help leaders understand the best ways to respond when a person 'comes out of the closet', revealing their struggle with SSA. You will gain an understanding of the spiritual bondage behind the practice of homosexuality and become able to provide practical solutions for ways to cope with same sex desires. You'll learn techniques to help those affected to fully comprehend the sin, while guiding them through repentance until they find complete healing and wholeness. One of the biggest questions in the church today is 'How do we reach people in the LGBTQ+ community—a community committed to protecting its bias toward sin with protests and shaming those who disagree?'

Another core question that follows is 'How have we as the body of Christ gotten it wrong by only recognizing the sin and not the person struggling with it? What can we do about it now?' To answer these questions, we first have to understand how the wrong approach contributed to the divide between the LGBTQ+ community and the body of Christ. Then, we will be able to correct our mistakes by executing the 'how to' concepts outlined in this Guide thereby building a better methodology.

Although these two groups' belief systems often oppose each other, we must learn to approach conversations of diverse perspectives with respect and respond with truth and love. Truth without Love does harm and Love without Truth creates lies. We can no longer stand silent on this topic or continue to avoid the subject simply because of the fear of confrontation. The cost of our silence will be the loss of countless souls to the enemy: Satan. We must instead expect confrontation and be prepared to respond with compassion. Recall that "A gentle answer turns away wrath, but a harsh word stirs up anger" (*Proverbs 15:11*). My hope is that as you read this Guide, you begin to develop that "gentle answer" while gaining general knowledge to assist in your interpretation of what the Bible says about homosexuality. Ultimately, you will learn how to minister to those influenced by a homosexual lifestyle with compassion and love, without compromising the Word of God.

The Stonewall Riots: The Root of the Gay Rights Movement

The Stonewall Riots are generally considered to be the catalyst for the modern Gay Rights Movement. In 1969, two men experiencing spiritual warfare in the realm of same sex attraction grew tired of being harassed by police and people in their New York City community. These two men decided to take a stand. Word of their demonstration spread throughout the City quickly inciting a riot. The protest quickly gained traction, other gay men and women joining in. They chanted a common phrase: 'gay power'. When police reinforcements arrived, they began to beat the crowd away. This riot inspired people with the same struggle throughout the country to unify in support of gay rights. Within two years after the riots, gay rights and groups had been formed in nearly every major city in the United States. If you're interested in finding out more, I encourage you to read more about The Stonewall Riots in your spare time.

After reading about the Stonewall Riots, I asked myself the following questions.

- **'What really started the gay rights movement?'**

- **'Was it a stand for gay people asking for permission to be gay?'** *or* **'Was it a group of human beings tired of being harassed for expressing or publicly showing their same sex attraction?'**

I don't want us to forget there was a time that when a person openly expressed their same sex attraction, they put themselves at risk of being beaten, thrown in jail, or even murdered. This is still happening today in many parts of the world. The Stonewall Riots demonstrated how gay individuals had to literally *fight* their way out of the condemnation placed on them by people who didn't know how to approach them. Instead of loving them, they beat them physically and emotionally. Instead of listening, they ignored them. Instead of finding ways to understand them to show them *the way out*, they treated them like outcasts.

Ultimately, via the actions of society at large, gay people came to believe that all they had was each other. I like to believe that when the LGBTQ+ community started the Gay Rights Movement, formerly called the Gay Liberation Movement, it was *not* to ask anybody permission to be gay or to force people to be gay. They were simply asking to be loved and accepted as human beings instead of being treated as subpar due to who they decided to be in a relationship with.

Though there are many differences, this is one reason why some compare the Gay Rights Movement to the Civil Rights Movement. These Movements share a common ground of abuse, harassment, and murder. In spite of the positive progress the LGBTQ+ community has accomplished to avoid being harassed, beaten, thrown in jail, and/or murdered due to publicly expressing same sex attraction, they have been deceived in the process of the Movement. This deception has blinded them. It has caused them to dismiss God's decrees and the fact that the practice of homosexuality is a sin in God's eyes!

What is the Practice of Homosexuality?

❖ A wise mentor once said "Homosexuality stems from a gender identity problem. It's not about sex!"

The practice of homosexuality occurs when a person, under the duress of unremitting and tormenting same sex desires, relinquishes their birth identity because they're unable to feel confident in it. It is a form of sexual brokenness deriving from emotional, mental, spiritual and/or relational trauma. It is Biblically categorized as sexual temptation, perversion and immorality. Despite what we've come to believe about homosexuality, it is a deeply rooted coping mechanism designed to compensate for our inability to embrace our original or birth gender.

Most people, however, are not taught to view homosexuality as a spiritual attack on their identity. Most believe it is who they are and how life was designed to be for them. If we begin, however, to teach people to spiritually view homosexuality as a gender issue, we can help them find freedom, healing and deliverance much earlier in their battle.

The Most Common Developmental Patterns of Homosexuality

Having listened to many testimonies, I've found that the testimony of Dr. Joseph Nicolosi and Melissa Fryrear best explain the correlations between one's relationship with their biological mother and father and one's developmental patterns. Impaired parental relationships are common in people struggling with homosexuality in this day of age. Keep in mind that there are individual variations within these patterns. Not everyone's journey is the same. As you read, I want you to think about the life experiences of people you may know who struggle with homosexuality or same sex attraction. Ponder on how their relationships with their parents play relevant roles in their respective behavioral patterns detailed herein.

Let's start with a typical male pattern. If you talk to a male who struggles with homosexuality, you will usually find the pattern of an unhealthy father and son relationship. This unhealthy pattern usually leads a boy to develop a strong relationship with his mother. A boy cannot learn to be a man from his mother. In some cases, a boy's mother is emotionally over-involved and has a strong, dominant personality. Meanwhile, the father is quiet, withdrawn, non-expressive and/or hostile. Men with a homosexual problem have not been emotionally nurtured or affirmed in their masculinity by their fathers. Although a boy's father may love him, something intercepted the son's perception of the love. The boy may often feel more comfortable in the company of other women as a result. Being feminine is familiar to him and being masculine is unfamiliar. His father didn't awaken masculinity in him. The boy is missing seeing the reflection of his own masculinity in his father. An emotional detachment takes place that's now carried over unto same sex peers.

Unable to come into his own masculinity, this boy will watch other boys while feeling inept or unable to join in the rough and tumble play that characterizes a boy's world. Staying on the fringes of boy culture, he looks with longing on the boys who remain unknown and elusive to him. What remains elusive and mysterious becomes eroticized during puberty. He gets excited by it and wants to be a part of it. There is, however, a psychological barrier that doesn't allow the boy to feel capable or equipped to do so. Then, envy sets in thereby creating the foundation for the cross-gender behavior.

For a little girl, bonding with her mother is important. A basic trust is built in a child between mother and daughter. If that foundation isn't well laid or a disruption occurs, then the little girl may fail to come into that sense of personal identity and sense of being. She may develop a sense of emptiness and longing. That inner sense of longing can manifest later in life through desires to want to connect via romantic relationships with other women. Thus, an overwhelming drive commences within to find her identity in the same sex other. It is a common pattern for women in same sex relationships to have experienced hurts from their mother.

Some women have mothers that are soft-spoken, well mannered, sincere, and kind. Yet, the daughter's perspective could be that mother was weak or ineffective. Some may feel misunderstood by their mother and they could never measure up to her expectations. They don't have to remember specific events that took place to cause this feeling. It is enough that they remember feeling a sense of displeasure from their mother. If a daughter perceives rejection from her mother, she begins to close her heart off to her mother. As the daughter begins to close her heart off, she drifts towards disconnecting from a painful consciousness of her femininity.

When core needs within a mother daughter relationship are not met, as characterized by a lack of emotional connection, a wedge comes between them. Instead of feeling a sense of attachment to her mother, detachment seeps in. Lack of intimacy engenders estrangement between them. Some women feel they never had a real, emotional connection with their mother. They seek that intimate relationship in every subsequent lesbian relationship.

A girl's father also has a crucial role to play in her life. He represents her first view of masculinity and therefore helps her learn how to interact with and relate to the opposite sex. If a girl grows up without a father or feels the father is not present enough, the girl will usually generalize that experience and expect the same from every man in her life. The deep pain of not receiving masculine value becomes a foundation for turning to women for comfort and valuation.

All girls need to know in some way that they are daddy's special little girls. Whether male or female, nobody chooses to have same sex attraction. But, in their quest to emotionally connect with their mother and father, they find themselves searching for this connection in the context of same sex relationships. Relationships with their mother and father can play a big part in their worth and value as well as how they interact with the opposite sex.

The following is a great question to ask the person you're working to help.

- **Can you describe the relationship you had with your biological mom and dad growing up?**

How Living in an Over-Sexualized Culture Can Play a Role in Homosexuality

Given how those within the LGBTQ+ community choose to define themselves, heartfelt compassion can lead us to want to allow these people that are often very beloved to us to simply live without opposition. The problem with this is that *not* challenging their deeply held confusion consigns them to a life where they cannot experience their true identity. But, they will only be able to access this if they are willing to walk all the way through God's healing process. Since sexuality and sexual activity have become highly normalized in music, media and television, modern culture has become highly sexualized. In fact, we've become somewhat desensitized portrayals of it.

In contrast with modern society, advertisements of the 1950's were much more modest. Showing too much skin or even a woman's leg was considered risqué. Until about the 1980's, if I'm not mistaken, sitcoms never really showed the bedroom. Networks would be fined if profanity made it on the air. In present day, it seems like almost anything goes. There is cursing in commercials, racy intimacy scenes on primetime TV, raunchy music videos, and scantily clad women on game shows, to name some examples. Displaying any same sex scenario was unheard of in the early years of media and entertainment.

As Dr. Joseph Nicolosi once stated "The media, movies, and TV always present the gay character as normal, well-adjusted, non-neurotic, wholesome, good looking, and at peace with himself, that they have it totally together." What they don't show, however, is the character who is heartbroken over failing to embody their gender. They've failed to embody their gender so much that they eventually succumb to believing they are indeed gay. Living in an over-sexualized culture has pushed individuals to sexualize homosexuality. This has made homosexuality about sex and not about sin. Looking from a spiritual lens, the act of homosexuality is influenced by more than just attractions alone. Ultimately, the issue lies in the developmental pattern of how one sees oneself.

How we interact with other people is a clear reflection of how we see ourselves. A person that practices homosexuality doesn't see themselves through the lenses of their Creator God, how He intended for them to function. We know that sex is one of the highest levels of communication you can have with a person. Sex can create unexplainable bonds between the two people involved. Most that have been delivered from homosexuality will reveal that, in the end, their sexual encounters did not fulfill their other needs. The battle of homosexuality is mental, not sexual. The mental torment of not knowing who you are is very, very hard to grasp. While looking in the mirror you see one thing but, ultimately, you feel and perceive something totally different. What you feel doesn't line up with what you're looking at and you don't know why or where these feelings came from. Every person practicing homosexuality has recognized this disconnection within themselves long before they were influenced to link it to homosexuality. Their identity issue started long before entering into a homosexual lifestyle.

A person goes through most of their life suffering through mental attacks against self that have caused them to have a very discouraging view of themselves. This skewed their perception of identity as a whole. When they found the option of same sex attraction and homosexual relationships, they concluded that could be the solution to the mental battle they had been secretly fighting. The moment they have sex with someone of the same sex, they found a way to justify their perception of self. Sex became more then just an act and became the ultimate level of justification on how they saw and define their identity.

Think about this for a moment. What is homosexuality without sex? Without sex, what are all the other issues you recognize within the LGBTQ+ community? Now take that into your prayer closet and God will reveal how homosexuality is not about sex but how one has a very interrupted, skewed perception of self.

How Gender Bias Can Play a Role in Homosexuality

One of the problems in present society is that we confine gender roles within stereotypically narrow definitions. For example, there should be latitude for men to be gentle and empathetic and for women to be decisive and competent. We should allow personal individuality to not define one's gender but encourage people to be fully expressive. For Athletically gifted girls, choosing to play basketball, join wrestling, or skateboard in place of activities largely perceived as feminine such as cheerleading, modeling, or ballet, this can be a challenge. They are generally viewed as tomboys.

When we refer to girls as tomboys solely because of their interest in activities that are more oriented towards masculinity, such as sports, it tends to plant seeds of homosexuality in her psyche. This labeling opens the door for suggestions that she's a girl who acts and thinks like a boy. As she grows, she may inadvertently begin to feel like she's never completely identified and been affirmed as a girl, given the emphasis on her interests. She may even choose to play the part others have affirmed the most, leading her to pursue becoming a 'real boy'. A boy who likes the arts, such as dance and theatre, or even one who takes extra care with his personal upkeep or is into style and fashion will be labeled as soft, sensitive, sissy, or gay. This can subsequently undermine his developing sense of manhood at a crucial age and later cause him to find someone who appreciates him as he is—even if it's through unhealthy or unnatural ways.

Here are some good questions to ask.

- **Girls: Where you labeled a tomboy growing up?**

- **Boys: Were you labeled as too soft growing up?**

Most people involved in homosexual lifestyles were not properly affirmed or categorized in how they expressed themselves within their realm of interests.

What is the LGBTQ+ or Gay Agenda?

The gay rights agenda is *not* about civil rights! It's about reconstructing the factors that differentiate male-ness and female-ness. LGBTQ+ activists propose that the terms 'male' and 'female' can be individually defined. They're trying to redefine 'male' and 'female', concepts that are fundamental to all aspects of our human experience.

Here are basic problems with homosexuality.

- **Homosexual intercourse cannot lead to procreation.**

- **Homosexuality doesn't produce life.**

- **Homosexual intercourse represents an affront to God's design of male and female.**

- **Homosexual conduct is contrary to and against nature.**

- **Homosexuality is a self-degrading behavior that dishonors the self.**

- **Homosexuality numbs the real pain of root issues.**

The Main LGBTQ+ Symbol

Apostle Paul tells us in *Romans 1:30* that society will *invent* ways of doing evil. I've outlined some of these invented ways below. These ways are propelling man-made gender identities at an alarming rate. By changing definitions and using terms with positive connotations, the LGBTQ+ community has rewritten the symology of being gay. For example, let's examine *the Rainbow*. The rainbow was never intended to be a sign of sexuality. Sadly when most see the rainbow, they think of the LGBTQ+ movement or gay people and not the promise of God written in *Genesis 9:13:* "I have set my rainbow in the clouds, and it will be the sign of the covenant between me and the earth."

The LGBTQ+ community has tried to give new meaning to the rainbow in the following ways.

- **Red: life**

- **Orange: healing**

- **Yellow: sunlight**

- **Green: nature**

- **Blue: harmony**

- **Purple: spirit**

    The misuse of this symbol is blasphemy of God's Word. Just because the LGBTQ+ community wears the rainbow benignly across their chest doesn't make what they are doing less dangerous. In fact, this twisting is encouraging young people to check out or test the gay lifestyle because it presents the potential for a gay or 'happy', colorful and entertaining life.

Unspoken Dangers, Warnings and Lies

Same sex relationships may look fun and glamorous *but* they have a high incidence of…

- **Physical, sexual, mental and emotional abuse**

- **Drug and alcohol abuse**

- **Disease (HIV and other sexually transmitted illnesses)**

- **Emptiness and endless searching for 'true love'**

The biggest lie in the LGBTQ+ community is that one cannot be delivered from homosexuality and that, once you're gay, you will always be gay.

Terms and Definitions

The terms and definitions listed below were created within and adopted by the LGBTQ+ community.

LGBTQ+ is an abbreviation or acronym used within the community to distinguish between the various categories they've invented. These categories may describe lesbian, gay bisexual, transgender, queer, questioning, intersex, and ally, as well as other gender and romantic identities. None of these categories are Biblical or defined by God, but based solely on sinful romantic, sexual, and gender attractions or preferences. They illustrate the ways in which the enemy is trying to distort, confuse, and eliminate the men and women God has lovingly and mindfully created. We never identify a person by these terms. But, by learning the terms, it could help you understand what area the person struggles with the most if they identify with one of the following.

Asexual or Ace: Experiencing little or no sexual attraction to others and/or a lack of interest in sexual relationships or behavior

Bigender: A person whose gender identity fluctuates between multiple genders, identifying with two or more genders

Bisexual or Bi: A person who is emotionally, romantically and/or physically attracted to two genders

Cisgender: A person whose gender identity and sex assigned at birth align

Demiromantic: A type of grey-romantic who only experiences romantic attraction after developing an emotional connection beforehand

Demisexual: A person who does not experience sexual attraction unless they form a strong emotional connection with someone. It's more commonly seen in, but by no means, confined to romantic relationships

Gay: Individuals who are primarily emotionally, romantically, and/or physically attracted to members of the same sex and/or gender

Gender Identity: One's own innermost concept of their gender. This is separate from gender expression and sexual or romantic orientation

Gender Non-conforming: A person whose gender expression and/or gender identity do not correspond with societal expectations of gender norms and roles

Genderqueer: Conveys a wider, more flexible range of gender expressions or identities, with interests and behaviors that may change from day to day

Pansexual, Panromantic, or Pan: A person who experiences emotional, romantic, physical, and/or spiritual attraction for members of all gender identities/expressions

Queer: A historically negative slur that is now reclaimed to identify LGBTQ folks as an umbrella term

Skoliosexual or Skolioromantic: A person who is primarily physically, romantically and/or emotionally attracted to genderqueer and/or non-binary people

Transgender or Trans: A person whose gender identity is different than that which they were assigned at birth

Nonbinary: A person whose gender identity isn't strictly male or female. Not all non-binary people identify as transgender

Intersex: This term describes a person with a rare combination of hormones, chromosomes, and anatomy. Intersex identified individuals were previously referred to as hermaphrodites or 'congenital eunuchs'.

In 19th and 20th century medical literature, intersex was referred as true hermaphroditism, female pseudo-hermaphroditism, and male pseudo-hermaphroditism reflecting the first taxonomic efforts to classify intersex conditions. These terms are no longer used. Terms including the word 'hermaphrodite' are largely considered misleading, stigmatizing, and scientifically erroneous.

A hermaphrodite is now defined as 'an animal or plant having both male and female reproductive organs'. People will often bring into discussion people born with abnormal chromosomes living out homosexual lifestyles. But, abnormal chromosomes do not mean these individuals were destined to be gay from birth.

This birth defect usually renders the person afflicted sterile but it has nothing to do with same sex attraction. Intersex individuals, first known as hermaphrodites, should not be placed amongst the LGBTQ+ community's collection of false identities. Intersex individuals' conflicts stem from physiological medical issues.

Some born with sexual birth defects may choose to identify by what they see on the outside like a counterfeit hundred dollar bill. If you hold it up to the light and compare it to a real bill, however, you will see the counterfeit bill is missing a watermark. The absence of a watermark proves the counterfeit bill is indeed counterfeit—that it wasn't manufactured through the proper authorities.

You can get away with spending counterfeit money in some places but truth is you can't get away with it in all places. You have to search for the weaker stores and crowds wherein you can get away with providing it and sell it for more than it's worth. You aim to collect real money with real value.

This can be compared to a person who believes God created them to be gay and uses their birth defect as a license to say they were born gay. This lie is worth no more than the paper counterfeit money is printed on. Anything outside original birth male or female, even if it resembles these genders, was not approved by the proper Creative Authority: God.

Those that identify with using one of the given terms operate in a counterfeit mindset, no matter what they do or say to justify their actions and who they are. Just like that counterfeit bill, when you examine their identity closely with God's light, you will see that it's counterfeit and can't be spent everywhere. So, whatever a person in the LGBTQ+ community may *look* like, sound like, or feel like on the surface, upon close examination, you can will see their real, God-given DNA.

Gay Pride

Gay pride parades are outdoor events celebrating lesbian, gay, bisexual, transgender, and questioning individuals' culture and pride. These events also at times serve as demonstrations for legal rights such as same sex marriage and other bills under the Sexual Orientation Gender Identity bills, also known as SOGI Laws. SOGI Laws are particular bills that people in the LGBTQ+ community and their allies are fighting for States to pass. These bills would allow for the state that passes them to take you're your son or daughter and allow someone else to adopt them if you do not allow your child to embrace a false identity or practice homosexuality.

Gay pride is a clear representation of *Proverbs 16:18*: "Pride goes before destruction, a haughty spirit before a fall." Even in their feeble attempts to change God's Truth, the LGBTQ+ community has failed to realize that there aren't actually any *new* genders being created—just made up words that combine, eliminate or in some way fuse the only two sexes that existed in the first place.

As much as we like to try to label our ability as human beings to define ourselves as *choice*, there still only exists two biological genders to choose from: XX (Female) and XY (Male). Even those who undergo massive hormone therapy can only hope to arrive at a place where they can only resemble another gender. They cannot change their DNA. The moment a transgender-identified person stops taking hormones or testosterone, their body will begin to revert back to its natural development process. The hormones and testosterone are put in place to confuse the body not transform it permanently or recreate new DNA.

Although there is a very big difference mentally between an individual battling transgenderism then just homosexuality we can somewhat use the same approach to reach both. Consequently, these terms can be a great distraction, especially in ministry. With the LGBTQ+ using so many terms many may focus on learning more about what these terms mean and where they came from rather than focusing on the ministry moment.

God wants to go to the heart of the matter, ministering to their ability to embrace their original identity. This allows you to come alongside of them for accountability. The terms they have invented are of very little importance. Regardless of how they define themselves or signs they use to justify this definition, all terms mentioned above fall under the same umbrella: sin that leads to death. The fact of the matter is that, without the terms outlined above, these individuals don't know who they really are. Again, remember that homosexuality stems from an identity problem first. It grows into a sexual perversion stronghold.

What Does the Bible Say About Homosexuality?

In this section I want to examine the theology or what the Bible says about the subject of homosexuality. This is *not* how I would initially approach a person who is struggling with homosexuality or same sex attraction. Please don't make the mistake of making this section your go to during the first approach to helping someone see *the way out*. My purpose in this section is to bring clarity to what the Bible says on the subject. In the body of Christ, I think it's important that we have methods of pastoring and counseling people who are having struggles.

I believe, however, that before we can show anybody *the way out* we need to make sure that we understand what the Bible says. Once we gain an understanding, we can develop strategies, ministries and approaches to helping people with this struggle. Don't take these Scriptures to a person and say these Scriptures will fix everything because it won't you might lose a friendship or a church member if these Scripture are the first thing you use to approach a person with this struggle.

Most, if not all, theological and ethical discussions of same sex relationships are based roughly on six Bible Verses. The LGBTQ+ community especially labels these as 'clobber

Verses' *Genesis 19:1-38*, *Leviticus 18:22* and *20:13*, *1 Corinthians 6:9-10*, *1 Timothy 1:9-10*, *Jude 6-7*, *Romans 1:25-27*. these Verses are frequently cited in a condemning manner at anyone who is trans, gay, lesbian, in a same sex relationship, or anyone who supports the LGBTQ+ community. For the sake of bringing clarification, I will attempt to help you understand that these Verses only become 'clobber Verses' after they have been grossly misinterpreted and carelessly generalized.

In this Guide, I will take a closer look at the 'clobber Verses' including one of my own found in *Deuteronomy 22:5*. I will examine these Verses and explain why these Verses are not 'clobber Verses'. Through examining these Verses, I hope to help shed light on the position people put themselves in with God if they continue to give themselves over to this sin. We know that these Scriptures should not be used to condemn but to show Truth. The fact they're considered 'clobber Verses' is due to the legalistic or condemning tone they've been presented to the LGBTQ+ community as well as hypersensitivity of the LGBTQ+ community.

Let's examine:
- *Genesis 19:1-38:* <u>Explanation:</u> This Verse is included in the 'clobber Verses'. Here, we'll focus on Verses four to seven. I encourage you, however, to read this chapter in its entirety to gain a complete understanding.

Verses four to seven say: "Before they had gone to bed, all the men from every part of the city of Sodom—both young and old—surrounded the house. They called to Lot, 'Where are the men who came to you tonight? Bring them out to us so that we can have sex with them.' Lot went to meet them and shut the door behind him and said, 'No, my friends. Don't do this wicked thing.'" This Scripture is self-explanatory; it supports the fact that homosexuality is a wicked practice. Therefore, I will not be breaking this Scripture down further in this Guide.

Let's examine:
- *Jude 6-7*: Explanation: This verse is included in the 'clobber Verses' but it may be the least used verse of the six when it comes to addressing homosexuality from a Biblical standpoint. The reason is that it is the most obscure Verses, being that it does not directly reference homosexuality. I do not break this verse down in this Guide.

Let's examine:
- *Leviticus 18:22* and *Leviticus 20:13*:
Leviticus 18:22: "Do not have sexual relations with a man as one does with a woman; that is *detestable.*" *Leviticus 20:13*: "If a man has sexual relations with a man as one does with a woman, both of them have done what is

detestable. They are to be put to death; their blood will be on their own heads."

Explanation: These Scriptures are included in the 'clobber Verses'. Although these Scriptures are found in the Old Testament, they outline the position a person puts themselves in by practicing homosexuality. It also illustrates the way God feels about it and how choosing to do so leads to eternity in hell. By defining what they've done as "detestable", the Scripture is not referencing the individual to be such. It outlines their choice to engage romantically or sexually with others of the same gender as perverted and detestable before God.

While other versions use the word 'abominable' or 'abomination', which is an extreme disgust or hatred, it is very important to ensure a person knows God does not hate them, but hates their choice of a same sex oriented lifestyle. The word 'detestable' is used in both *Leviticus 18:22* and *Leviticus 20:13*. In Hebrew the word 'to-e-vah' is translated as 'abomination'. There is widespread agreement amongst Hebrew scholars that the word 'toevah' as used in Leviticus is not, in fact, a moral term. Instead, it is a cultic term that indicates 'ritual uncleanness'.

Let's examine:
- *Deuteronomy 22:5*: "A woman must not wear men's clothing, nor a man wear women's

clothing, for the Lord your God *detests* anyone who does this."

Explanation: This Scripture's main context is not addressing clothing. It digs deeper into how a man should not take on the characteristics of a woman and how a woman should not take on the characteristics of a man. When we view *Deuteronomy 22:5* in the right context, one is able to discern God's ordinances. You can *see* what happens with people dealing with cross gender confusion.

A man wearing women's clothing begin to act or appear more feminine. A woman may wear men's clothing and act or appear more masculine. While clothes are not the primary concern, they parallel how they make the person feel (i.e. a man like a woman, and woman like a man).

God's issues with gender appropriation through clothing lie mostly in that wearing the opposite gender's clothing causes a person with identity issues to associate their emotions and self-perception with that gender. Clothing has deeply associated emotions and connotations, and expectations people naturally assign to it.

For those who don't recognize the significance of modifying wardrobe to reflect gender, help them understand the connection between the way they dress and act. Dressing like the opposite sex encourages one to take on the behaviors and body language of that gender, which can stifle growth by attracting familiar spirits, unwanted attention, old habits and patterns. Some may wear the opposite clothing as an armor to protect them from the opposite gender sexualizing them or victimization.

- *1 Corinthians 6:9-10*: It is included in the 'clobber Verses'. "Or do you not know that wrongdoers will not inherit the kingdom of God? Do not be deceived: Neither the sexually immoral nor idolaters nor adulterers nor men who have sex with men nor thieves nor the greedy nor drunkards nor slanderers nor swindlers will inherit the kingdom of God."

Explanation: I like this Scripture because most people living a homosexual lifestyle find ways to demonstrate how we all sin, but this particular passage doesn't let anyone slide. From idolatry and alcoholism to lying and stealing, the text illustrates how all who continue to choose wayward lifestyles will suffer the same fate.

By highlighting fairly common sins with which most people struggle, it doesn't single any one sin out. Also, it doesn't categorize one as better or worse than the other, but clearly states that all who willingly choose sin forfeit their inheritance—the kingdom of God. This includes sexual immorality, such as fornication and adultery as well as homosexuality.

The goal here is help them understand they're not being singled out in isolation, but grouped into an integrated sect of people who choose to continue living in various sinful ways. And the only way to achieve freedom is to focus on fixing their individual sinful desire of homosexuality and choose to walk away from the lifestyle it entails, including behaviors and activities that trigger it.

Help them understand why waiting for the world to change is not only the wrong focus because we live in a falling world, but a deceptive trick of the enemy that blocks the pathway to freedom—because in the end, everyone answers for themselves and this Scripture shows that no one is exempt from the consequences of their personal choices.

- *1 Timothy 1:10.* This Verse is also included in the 'clobber Verses'. Explanation: This verse contains a list of vices that is very similar to *1 Corinthians 6:9-10.* Therefore, I will not go into detail about it.

- *Romans 1:18-32*: This Verse is also included in the 'clobber Verses'. Explanation: This is an extensive amount of Scripture that I encourage you to read and examine at your leisure.

Let's especially focus on:

- *Romans 1:25-32*: "They exchanged the truth about God for a lie, and worshiped and served created things rather than the Creator—who is forever praised. Amen. Because of this, God gave them over to shameful lusts. Even their women exchanged natural sexual relations for unnatural ones. In the same way the men also abandoned natural relations with women and were inflamed with lust for one another. Men committed shameful acts with other men, and received in themselves the due penalty for their error. Furthermore, just as they did not think it worthwhile to retain the knowledge of God, so God gave them over to a depraved mind, so that they do what ought not to be done. They have become filled with every kind of wickedness, evil, greed and depravity. They are full of envy, murder, strife, deceit and malice. They are gossips, slanderers, God-haters, insolent, arrogant and boastful; they invent ways of doing evil; they disobey their parents; they have no understanding, no fidelity, no love, no mercy. Although they know God's righteous decree that those who do such things deserve death, they not only continue to do these very things but also approve of those who practice them."

Explanation: This passage lets us know what we're dealing with when a person is living a homosexual lifestyle and fails to retain the knowledge of God. It reminds us that that they've fallen into a futile or depraved mindset and that God has given them over to their unnatural desires after they *choose* not to retain the knowledge of God.

This also leads them to subconsciously become filled with all kinds of wickedness, such as envy, murder, strife, deceit and malice. They tend to become gossipers, slanderers, God-haters, insolent, arrogant and boastful. They are being influenced to invent ways of doing evil. God brings much revelation just reading and thinking of gay pride and how the LGBTQ+ community speaks about the church and anyone who disagrees with their lifestyle.

When someone comes out the closet as gay, we must look beyond the same sex desire expressions to see the spiritual attack on the individual. If we can't do this, we mislead them and ourselves. We have to see and hear the spiritual bondage attached to their confession, while discerning the spirit behind what they're not saying—even if they're unaware of the way that it's discussed in *Romans 1*.

Consider the following scenario. A person approaches you coming out the closet. Instead of hearing 'Hello, I'm gay.' What if you heard 'Hello, I'm becoming filled with a spirit of every kind of wickedness, I'm evil, I'm greedy, and I'm developing a depraved mindset. I'm also full of envy, murder, strife, deceit, and malice. I gossip,

I'm a slanderous person, I'm a God-hater, I'm insolent, arrogant and boastful. And, I invent ways of doing evil... Nice to meet you.'

If we were honest, most people would be extremely alarmed. Yet, this is the level of attack on those that are battling and accepting of homosexuality. Those that are not accepting of it should know that they are being mentally and emotionally tormented by all of these demonic spiritual influences. So, if we're going to truly understand how to help them and what to pray for, we must open our spiritual eyes when a person 'comes out of the closet' declaring 'I am gay.'

The LGBTQ+ community studies these Scriptures and takes what seems to be a clear statement and presents it from many different angles to throw doubt into your mind. They present them differently from how the Bible states. It creates doubt in your heart until your not sure if what the Bible is saying is what it's actually saying. This is how the LGBTQ+ community goes after dismantling these Scriptures. They use them out of their proper context.

They often say counter healthy interpretations of Scripture with the following arguments.

- **Does the Old Testament Law apply to Christianity today?**

- What about eating pork and shellfish?

- What about wearing mixed fabric?

- Weren't these the Laws used to enforce the system of patriarchy?

- **Homosexuality described in the Bible is related to idolatry, idol worship or homosexual expression that is exploitive in nature. It does not comment on the loving, monogamous side of homosexuality.**

My goal with this Guide is not teach you how to debate when objectives come but to point out the most common objectives you will hear when using these Scriptures so you can prepare your soft rebuttal during that time. With this Guide, my main goal is for you to gain a different perspective of what homosexuality is and no what the world has made it out to be. Our problem is not in understanding if homosexuality is a sin our problem lays in how do we approach and help someone with this struggle identify homosexuality as sin and not their God-giving identity.

Understanding the Spiritual Influences Behind Homosexuality

❖ *Ephesians 6:12-13*: "For our struggle is not against flesh and blood, but against the rulers, against the authorities, against the powers of this dark world and against the spiritual forces of evil in the heavenly realms. Therefore put on the full armor of God, so that when the day of evil comes, you may be able to stand your ground…"

We have to teach people to separate the practice of homosexuality from the person. Homosexuality is not the person. It's the sexual behavior they are practicing. His/her spiritual strongholds are rooted in brokenness. These may include, but certainly aren't limited to influences from spirits of lust, promiscuity, rage, perversion, pride, confusion, fear and idolatry. They can enter a person's life through open doors of unaddressed issues of rejection, abandonment, resentment or unforgiveness. They can influence a person to entertain or engage in the homosexual lifestyle, preventing them from finding freedom through God.

However, we must be mindful that this type of bondage can be extremely tormenting for the one battling it. They may not be able to distinguish between the spiritual influence and his or her actual self. When helping someone overcome these strongholds, the goal is to get to the root issue and figure out where the door was opened that allowed these demonic influences to take hold. Once establishing trust, it is important to begin to understand what some of the issues they secretly battled with before coming out were and, in some cases, still secretly battling with.

Please understand that being gay is never the root issue. It's always the result of root issues. A person desiring freedom must gain the courage to address the root issues in their heart. As they began to see their homosexual/transgenderism behavior as a coping mechanism born out of their deep hunger for same gender parent nurture or other unpleasant events, they will become able to challenge their behavior.

Can a Person Be Born Gay?

❖ *Proverbs 23:7 (KJV)*: "For as he thinketh in his heart, so is he". The Bible proves if a man thinks of his self a certain way long enough, he will began to believe what he thinks and act according to those thoughts.

Please note that if a person continually repeats their opinion that they were born gay, you do not need to debate this endlessly. Simply request that they read *John 3:3*: "Jesus replied, "Very truly I tell you, no one can see the kingdom of God unless they are born again." Such a person that argues they were born gay or solely base their identity using one of the terms giving, is double-minded and unstable in all they do. We have to be prepared to restore them gentle as we lead them back to recognize their true identity.

Some people mistakenly believe that a 'gay gene' has been discovered. Despite the huge amount of money and time professionals have spent searching for this evidence, the fact is they have not been able to find one shred of biological or scientific evidence for this theory. Everyone is born their biological gender, but some fail to embody or take it on. Even rare exceptions such as intersex individuals have a genetic code and/or reproductive organs that indicates what their God-ordained gender should be recognized as.

We must remember that all behavior has a root basis. We may not choose our personal challenges but we *do* choose how we respond to them.

Nobody *chooses* to be attracted to the same sex. People *do choose* whether to *act* on those desires. Despite the popular theories surrounding the issue, no one is *born* gay. However, a person can be enticed or even experience romantic or sexual feelings and thoughts towards members of the same sex for as long as they can remember. The reason for this is that gender formation begins to formulate by approximately the age of three. Ask any normally developing three-year old the question 'What is your gender?'. You will receive a shocked look and emphatic reply along the vein of 'I am a girl!' or 'I am a boy!'

For the individual that is experiencing gender confusion at an early age, they've begun to feel like they don't belong. They may recall the uncomfortable feeling of these attractions, before they're even able to psychologically conceptualize the meaning of what they're feeling. They look to their parents, teachers, friends and the world around them to give meaning to how they feel. These are children who experience gender distress early. They are often called gay based on their mannerisms or interests, even before they understand what gay means. The child may eventually begin to identify their feelings or interests with labels such as gay, faggot, or dyke.

This identification opens the door to a lifestyle they may not necessarily want.

The enemy can also use different tricks to play on these feelings through peers, bullying and media. In attempts to increase the intensity of the feelings, Satan will try to infiltrate the child's mind through dreams, planting images of engaging in sexual acts with the same gender, or even dressing as or becoming the opposite gender. This can create a desire to act on how they feel or re-enact the images they see, making the temptation to embrace these attractions harder to resist. These impressions, various messages, and temptations can cause the adolescent to conclude 'I must have been born gay'.

It's extremely important for the body of Christ, especially youth group workers, to become equipped to explain the root causes for their attraction to these individuals before they take on a gay identity. Without this crucial support, the young person that is struggling with temptations may feel the only place they can find acceptance is in the LGBTQ+ affirming community. This following question is a good one to ask. 'At what age where you introduced to porn or any sexual activities like masturbation and visualizing yourself with the same gender?'

I think the strong belief that homosexuality is genetic or biological is because homosexual development can start at a very early age and it can't be fixed by any manmade drugs and there's no from of therapy that can remove the attraction one has towards the same sex. In some cases, not even resisting can take away this attraction. The emotion is so real it can cause a critical interruption in the developing pattern of how one views themselves and their identity. This leaves them to define themselves by their attraction alone. The sole cure for homosexuality is found when a person surrenders their life to Christ no matter how they feel as well as the supernatural drawing of the Holy Spirit.

Without these two, no one can be delivered form homosexuality or learn to endure the tormenting stronghold of having a same sex emotional attraction. Homosexuality is not something you fix. It's something you surrender to God. It's the only thing in the Bible that's referred to as unnatural. This means that, in order to be changed, a person has to be willing to repent. This way, they can respond to the convictions of a supernatural encounter that comes only from God revealing Scripture or by way of the Holy Spirit. Outside of Jesus, it's impossible to overcome homosexuality. There's no AA meeting for homosexuality helping you avoid, get away from, or manage an emotion you didn't ask for.

What Does a Person Mean When They Say They Were 'Born Gay'?

❖ *Isaiah 3:9:* "The look on their countenance is witness against them, And they declare their sin as Sodom; They do not hide it. Woe to their soul! For they have brought evil upon themselves"

What these individuals are truly expressing is when they first *decided to act* on their homosexual desires. Many people feel a sense of great relief after 'coming out'. The cognitive dissonance is finally over. Many people report that it was when they owned their gay identity that they finally felt real, wanted, and/or loved for the first time. Before they ever outwardly expressed being gay, verbally or otherwise, they go through a psychological battle that traps them in a mindset with tormented emotions. This inspires them to believe they were born gay. They become stuck and begin to repeatedly ask themselves the following questions.

- **What am I?**

- **Who am I?**

- **Am I a boy or a girl?**

- **Why do I like my own gender?**

- **Did God make a mistake?**

These individuals grow to believe they found the answers to their existence once they come out. Before coming out, they begin a secret search for answers to those questions. This is initially done in silence. At first, they really hate the same sex emotion and most don't want it. They feel shame because they innately sense it is not God's natural design. They desperately want to understand and gain some type of control of what they're feeling because being held captive in your mind and body is both uncomfortable and unpopular.

Coming out of the closet seems to resolve this long-standing dilemma for them. In order for someone to come out of a closet, they must first feel they're trapped in one. They do not know how to express what they feel outside of sexual contact with the same gender. Any mention of salvation sounds like an attempt to make them go back into the very closet from which they feel like they have escaped from. This is the reason why the church must understand what they have been going through, compassionately commit to walking with them, and to showing them *the way out*.

One cannot concurrently *identify* as homosexual and a Christian. Identification with

Christ must displace identity based on desire that does not conform to God's Word. "Therefore, if anyone is in Christ he is a new creation; old things have passed away; behold, all things have become new." *(2 Corinthians 5:17)*.

How to Open Conversation with Someone Who Believes They Were Born Gay

Having an open and respectful attitude is very important. People will only confide in others who want to understand them and are not just trying to change them. It is important to establish trust in the relationship, and not try to go too fast. Being able to listen with empathy and asking questions like this will help them begin to unpack their story.

- **Do you remember the first time you recognized you had a same sex attraction?**

- **How long did it take for you to sexually act out on that emotion with someone of the same sex?**

- **Did you try to find answers to your same sex desires by exploring sexual activities with people of the opposite gender before coming out?**

- **What thought process encouraged you to hold these desires in and not act on it when you first felt the desire?**

- Do you recall any significant events going on at the time when you started to recognize your same sex attractions? If so, what were those events? Divorce, rape, bullying, molest station, continuous mistreatment by the opposite gender etc.

- Have you experience sexual abuse or sexual play from the same sex or opposite gender?

- What specific event took place that convinced you to believe you no longer had to feel shame or hide these emotions?

- How did you feel after coming out?

- Did any of your root insecurities change after coming out?

Asking questions will help you understand how long they had felt tormented before choosing to outwardly express their struggle. This will also point to a type of discomfort they experienced that stopped them from acting on it immediately. Often people will have an initial sense of shame, or that something is wrong with their desires. We want to know more about what was going on before they came out. This reveals the roots of things that pushed them to embrace a homosexual lifestyle and what caused them to exchange the Truth they once acknowledged for a lie.

Preparing Leaders of the Church

❖ *James 3:1:* "Not many of you should become teachers, my fellow believers, because you know that we who teach will be judged more strictly."

As a leader, we must learn to balance Truth and love. Love heals and affirms (*1 Corinthians 13:4-7*). Truth makes one free (*John 8:31-32*). The following are things the church should consider when interacting with the LGBTQ+ community.

- **Prepare the congregation on how to interact with the LGBTQ+ community.**

- **Do *not* avoid entering into relationship with them. Embrace and get to know them.**

- **Do *not* compromise your belief in Biblical Truth. Stand firm on the Word of God.**

"For the word of God is alive and active. Shaper than any double-edge sword, it penetrates even to dividing soul and spirit, joints and marrow; it judges the thoughts and attitudes of the heart. Nothing in all creation is hidden from God's sight. Everything is uncovered and laid bare before the eyes of him to whom we must give account." (*Hebrews 4:12-13*).

As a leader, it is important to gain basic knowledge about homosexuality and its spiritual influences. But also understand that, when someone struggling with homosexuality attends your church for the first time, they typically interact with members of the congregation as opposed to those in leadership. Depending on how they're treated by those with whom they come in contact, they'll likely judge the church leader and God based on that encounter. When most people come to church, they're not searching for Jesus. They're simply searching for someone they can relate to or to understand them without feeling judged.

Therefore, it's very important to make sure your congregation not only understands what the Bible says about homosexuality, but that your members are in tune with the ways in which they're expected to treat those who may be struggling and considering your church as a potential place of worship. *The way out* of homosexuality is not an easy process. The way to make it easiest for those struggling is to love them, provide reliable support and help them build a relationship with Christ through understanding God's Word. Give them time to learn worship and fall in love with Jesus as they assemble with the saints.

What Do I Do if They Want to Lead in the Church?

Should a practicing adulterer be allowed to lead the church? Should a known liar be allowed to govern the church? Should a person walking in willful disobedience lead the body? No! According to *1 Timothy 3:1-7,* there are qualifications for Overseers and Deacons.

First Timothy 3:1-7: "Here is a trustworthy saying: Whoever aspires to be an overseer desires a noble task. Now the overseer is to be above reproach, faithful to his wife, temperate, self-controlled, respectable, hospitable, able to teach, not given to drunkenness, not violent but gentle, not quarrelsome, not a lover of money. He must manage his own family well and see that his children obey him, and he must do so in a manner worthy of full respect. (If anyone does not know how to manage his own family, how can he take care of God's church?) He must not be a recent convert, or he may become conceited and fall under the same judgment as the devil. He must also have a good reputation with outsiders, so that he will not fall into disgrace and into the devil's trap."

First Timothy 3:1-7 doesn't imply that they can't be used. But, they must not be placed in a position of leadership. Alternatively, they can join small groups and other ministries that allow them to fellowship with the body in order to grow and learn how to interact with people in a new and healthy way. They can bring food, put up chairs, and clean up after meetings just like any other believer in process of transition. People that identify as gay are still people. They function just as well as any other human being trying to get their life in order.

It is wise to find a way to keep them connected to the body without putting them in leadership due to a well known talent or gift you discover before they summit to God's will. Know the difference between a person struggling and a person giving themselves to their struggle and attempting to deceive the church into allowing them to have a leadership role. A Pastor has the right to remain abreast of the life affairs within church and outside of church for anybody that wants to be in leadership. Everybody has a place in the body of Christ. You have to help them find their place no matter where they are when they decide to join your church.

Introduction of Their Homosexuality: Trauma and Choice

To get to the root of how or why someone believes they are homosexual, we must *listen* to them and explore the three main identifiers in their story: trauma, choice or exposure. The term(s) they have adopted to define themselves is irrelevant. Everyone that has fallen into the temptation of same sex attraction has a story that begins with one of the above three identifiers. Everyone has had different mental, emotional, and social reactions to whatever event(s) caused them to believe they had to practice homosexuality to discover their true identity. When listening to their story, you want to listen for these three main identifiers (trauma, choice, or exposure) to find the pieces to their puzzle. Let's examine each of these three identifiers.

Trauma: A lasting shock resulting from an emotionally disturbing experience or physical injury.

Common types of trauma:

- **Childhood abandonment**

- Childhood abuse (emotional, mental, physical and/or sexual)

- Divorce

- Parental rejection

- Bullying and/or teasing for not meeting the stereotypical gender roles

- Sibling rivalry

- Death of a close relative/friend

- Unhealthy or abusive relationships with opposite sex

- Incest

- Exposure to pornography

- Having a parent who wished they were the opposite gender

- Having an absent or neglectful parent

- Early childhood inner turmoil (being afraid of people taking shots at who they are)

- **Not being aroused or responding how their peers did when introduced to sex can impact one's identity. It can make one feel as if they failed a test when they didn't feel or respond how their peers did in certain situations towards the opposite sex regarding being aroused sexually or emotionally.**

Trauma opens the door to fear. For example, one may fear the person who perpetrated their trauma. They may apply this to all persons of the same gender. In turn, this may lead to a craving to have a co-dependent relationship or fantasies involving people of the same sex that affirm them in their natural gender. In turn, this may lead to a secret craving that develops into them having a co-dependent relationship.

Or, they can also develop fantasies about people of the same sex they look up to or want to be like. By doing this they create a false relationship with that person and, in some ways, fantasies about that person affirming them in the areas they seem to lack in their natural gender. When a person feels rejected in their natural gender, they crave it and that craving can become sexualized in the person they're seeking the most affirmation from.

People falling into this category use homosexuality to cope with the pain of their trauma. Many people who struggle with homosexuality are not aware of its connection to their childhood traumas or a disruption in their developmental pattern of how they view identity. Another way that homosexuality can be introduced to a child is through sexual play. This may not be recognized as traumatic. It is, however, a defilement and can introduce the child to a sexual spirit that gains a foothold in their life. Exploring each family relationship and any revealed patterns will help you understand their traumas.

<u>Choice</u>: For these individuals, being gay is entertaining. In these cases, homosexual practice is not a stronghold. This is most common in lesbian communities. Generally, this is seen with women who have had difficult or abusive relationship with men. They reach for emotional connection that they find in lesbian relationships.

<u>Key points to look for:</u>

- **Unhealthy or abusive relationships with opposite sex**

- **Phrases of belief akin to 'I'm only gay for the person I'm currently with.'**

- **Identifying as 'bisexual'**

The keys for the deliverance of these people lie in their understanding of their self-worth. They also depend on their development of healthier heterosexual relationships. They also need to recognize that God has placed boundaries on sexual expressions that result in harm. They need to be willing to obey God's boundaries for sexuality.

In 2006, a woman named Melissa Fryrear shared her testimony out of homosexuality. Through her story, God provided several common patterns I mention here. These are patterns of women who choose to practice homosexuality, as I have discerned are prevalent in the lesbian community.

1. **Most women in homosexuality experiment. They don't embrace a lesbian identity but just engage in experimenting with same sex behavior.**

2. **Emotional attachment. These are women who say they would never have sex with a woman and find the practice disgusting at first. The problem enters when they find themselves at a low place in life coupled with not having a sense of who they are as a person after experiencing several failed heterosexual relationships. She begins to**

rely on another woman to gain a sense of identity for herself. She has stepped into a co-dependent relationship that veers into homosexual practice.

3. Sometimes, the problem lies in her interaction with same sex peers as she grew up. She felt different, comparing herself to her peers. She never felt like she measured up. She feels different in some way, believing she will never measure up to whatever the expectations of femininity and womanhood are. In some way she feels that she's not meeting the mark. So, the question becomes 'Where do I fit in? I know I'm not a boy, but I don't feel like a woman either.' She then begins to withdraw from the group of people with whom she needs to spend her time with to continue to build to her identity as a woman.

4. In many cases, women can be identified as tomboys or mistaken for a boy at some point during their childhood.

5. When starting, lesbians have higher rates of promiscuity than heterosexual women. Their high levels of promiscuity are on par with the levels of promiscuity of some heterosexual men. These women tend to

have no sexual boundaries.

6. Some may feel that men only care about themselves and all they want is sex. Some feel they can't be trusted and are womanizers. Some feel a man could never love them like a woman could. As a result, a woman may dress like a man to hide her feminine image. This is an effort to protect herself from being recognized by a man or from being a victim of sexual abuse perpetrated by a man.

Sexual abuse amongst lesbian identified women is high in this group. Most have experienced some type of sexual abuse as a child. This could later propel them to practice homosexuality. Personally, I have never been sexually assaulted or abused by a man. Most women I talk to, however, have been sexually assaulted at some point in their lives. It is not always the case these women have been assaulted by men. In addition, some women have been sexually abused or assaulted by another woman. Similarly, men encounter sexual abuse from either other men or women.

Any abuse, especially sexual abuse, can have a long-term effect on the emotional behavior of that person. Some of those consequences could be guilt, shame, anxiety, lowered self-esteem, depression, venerability to drug and alcohol abuse.

Other consequences are impaired ability to judge trustworthiness of others, confusion between receiving and giving care, confusion about sexual identity and sexual norms, and an inability to differentiate sex from love. These are just a few factors. I don't think any of these are singular causes. They are, however, correlations we would be foolish to minimize or ignore when learning someone's story and how they developed same sex attraction.

Abuse can go on forever in the mind. People make inner vows that can leave an open door to homosexuality. Some of these vows are 'I won't allow another man to hurt me', 'Women are weak and gullible', 'I'll never get married', and 'I'll never let a man touch me'. We all have inner judgments in our lives based on good and bad experiences. Our perception of these experiences and resulting feelings inspire us to make the decisions we've made.

In abusive lesbian relationships, many will compare their negative experiences from guys and girls. In their relationships with women, they may feel women respond to their hurt differently from men. They may feel women understand them better than men. A woman is supposed to respond and understand another woman better than a man. Likewise, it is also the case that another man will generally understand a man better than a woman.

This is a part of the mystery God created in both genders and part of the fun in being in relationship with the opposite gender. Men can't compare the two by saying 'I had a better relationship with a man'. Women, on the other hand, can't compare the two by saying 'I had a better relationship with a woman'. Both genders have common emotions, but this doesn't negate their areas of distinction in ability to relate. Some men and women just don't know how to be attracted to the opposite sex. I can attest to that personally as I didn't find myself sexually attracted to men until the age of 26. This was still a year and a half after my deliverance from homosexuality. As I've come to understand who I am in Christ, I've learned that my identity should be defined beyond my sexual attractions.

Introduction of Their Homosexuality: Exposure

Exposure: Witnessing, experiencing, or being made susceptible to some kind of gay activity or person at an early age.

Struggling with homosexuality is a very common occurrence in individuals who grew up in a household run by gay parents. When children are exposed to homosexuality early on, it opens up the possibility to and sometimes even encourages them to label themselves as gay/bisexual and practice homosexuality. Those who become gay via exposure don't embark on a path of homosexuality due to battling a trauma or making a choice. They have watched someone living out or modeling a homosexual lifestyle. Depending on that modeler's level of influence in their lives, they can be inspired to mimic the modeler's actions and follow their lead into a homosexual lifestyle.

The Key to Helping Victims of Exposure

When children grow up around gay people, they don't see their influencers as gay people. These influences don't necessarily raise the children to be gay. These influences generally do not recognize the sin they perpetuate. The children only begin to wonder about the gay identity when they start hearing the comments of others regarding their environment and the types of people who they're surrounded by or are being raised by.

Without understanding what they're being exposed to, these children are subject to developing a false sense of identity of their own personhood. In *Luke 17:1-3*, Jesus said to his disciples: "Things that cause people to stumble are bound to come, but woe to anyone through whom they come. It would be better for them to be thrown into the sea with a millstone tied around their neck than to cause one of these little ones to stumble. So watch yourselves." A good discussion question to ask is 'Did you grow up seeing or interacting with or were you raised by gay identified individuals?

For those struggling with homosexuality due to exposure, it is important to point out to how their familiarity with the lifestyle at such a young age made them vulnerable. Specifically, highlight that their comfort in practicing homosexuality came from the exposure of what they saw others practice growing up. Ask them how and when they learned about sex or sexuality. Help them navigate through their past to understand *who* and *what* had the greatest influence on their decision to become homosexual. On the other hand, there are some children growing up with gay-identified parents who tend to have anger toward their gay identified parents that they cannot safely express. They have a longing to have a mother and a father and don't desire to have two fathers or two mothers.

Please know that even though each person starts with trauma, choice or exposure be mindful that, once involved in a homosexual lifestyle, they are subject to go through all three. For someone trying to overcome acting out on their same sex attraction, it's important for them to learn the root of their individual triggers, and begin to pay close attention to events that could initiate or even instigate the desire (i.e. a recent argument with a loved one, work stress, a break-up etc.).

Why Listening to Their Story is Important

1. It reveals to you what triggers led them to enter the practice of homosexuality (trauma, choice, or exposure).

2. It helps you get to know the person and shift your focus from the practice of homosexuality to the heart of the person. This helps you have more patience, love, and compassion for them.

3. It gives them a safe place to vent that many involved in homosexuality have never had outside the realm of judgment or acceptance without accountability.

4. It gives you the opportunity to offer specific practical tips for the person to do in their alone time to avoid dwelling in the past and to endure through moments of temptation.

5. It helps you pull each piece of their story together and show them where their strongholds took root. It also helps you understand why they felt they had to be gay.

6. It helps you understand why they may not

want to get out.

You have to help these individuals understand that God's opposition to homosexuality is not just about their living a sinful perverted life. There's reason(s), however, for the same sex attraction they're experiencing. We must help them learn how to get their emotional needs met and show them how to meet these needs on their own. Up until now, they been trying to do it sexually and they're coming to you because they are realizing that it's not working. They continue to feel the same hurt they felt before they stepped into practicing homosexuality. We want to show them how to obtain real healing.

Their healing can be found in having platonic relationships with other people of the same gender. This is about men bonding with men and women bonding with other women. They will discover the desire to act out some of those same sex desires will become endurable or fade away. Make sure they understand how they may feel little triggers of temptation during these interactions but, the more they bond with those of the same gender in nonsexual godly relationships, those triggers will die down or simply fade away. As you can see, there is not one single factor that contributes to homosexuality. It's an accumulation of factors.

Female homosexuality can be a bit more complex as there could be more of a fluctuation in sexuality, attractions and behaviors. This is something we don't see often in male homosexuality. Listening to a person's story is the best way to start the process of showing them *the way out*. Listening and providing loving feedback laced with God's Truth can give them hope that, as difficult as the journey may have been thus far, it's not over and it can end in victory. *Revelation 12:11* tells us "They triumphed over him by the blood of the lamb and by the word of their testimony; they did not love their lives so much as to shrink from death."

We want these individuals to understand that they only have a glimpse of their story in view. *Haggai 2:9* promises "…The glory of this present house will be greater then the glory of the former house' says the Lord Almighty. 'And in this place I will grant peace', declares the LORD Almighty." Individuals who are struggling have the part of their story that is devoid of God's presence. We want them to come to look forward to their story with God.

Ways to Educate Your Congregation

- Have a service, workshop, or Bible study gathering geared toward teaching your congregation how to love and approach those operating in homosexuality.

- Teach the church proper etiquette when around a person during their process of transformation. I can vividly remember that, during my transition, a woman pulled me into a room to pray over me and the same sex desires I was battling with at the time. She was wearing a top revealing so much cleavage that I couldn't receive her prayer.

- Create a ministry with people assigned to be accountability partners for those in homosexuality seeking *the way out*. It's good to know if there are members who have been delivered from homosexuality as well as those who may be silently struggling. If you know, you can arrange to meetings with them to have open dialogue. You can learn a lot from these individuals.

- Make sure your church understands where the Pastor stands when it comes to homosexuality while, at the same time, creating a friendly and loving place for the LGBTQ+ community.

- Generally preach about sexual sin in a way that does not highlight homosexuality as the worst kind of sexual sin. Also preach about what true identity looks like in Christ.

Understanding the Cost of One Walking Away From Their Lifestyle

These are common costs individuals pay to leave their lifestyle of homosexuality.

- **They will go through a process of grieving the loss of their false 'identity'.**

- **They have to learn to relate to people in a new way.**

- **They suffer the loss of their former 'community'.**

- **They enter a process of learning proper femininity and masculinity.**

The Unraveling Process of Healing

These are common aspects of the unraveling process of healing for individuals who choose to walk away from their lifestyles.

- **Practical support from the church (including modeling of appropriate ways to dress, mannerisms, counseling, and fellowship)**

- **Healing wounds that led to homosexuality**

- **Exposure to healthy families (Believers should welcome these individuals into their home, as led by the Holy Spirit, so they can see how the nature of 'family' operates. If you have small children, be careful with the amount of their exposure to cross dressers who may visit your home. Homosexuality is not contagious but can be very influential.)**

- **Dissolution of civil union, if applicable (adopted children may be involved)**

- **Sale of home(s) and property(ies) shared with former partner(s) while in lifestyle**

- **Movement away from all details pertaining to the past and pressing into the future**

    Armed with right information, we can approach those in this battle by bridging the gap with love and Truth. We must equip the saints to first get a general understanding of homosexuality, the spirit influencing those entangled, and the realities attached to leaving the lifestyle.

The Importance of Your Kind of Approach

> ❖ A wise mentor once said "When you approach a person influenced by a lifestyle of homosexuality, it should be an unexpected encounter that disarms them from every preceding experience that resulted in a wrong reaction to their emotional struggle."

After having lived a lifestyle of homosexuality for 13 years, two encounters completely changed the way I thought about myself as well as the LGBTQ+ community. Both encounters happened at Koinonia Christian Church in Arlington, Texas, to be exact. This is the church I now call my home church. On my second Sunday visiting, a lady by the name of Mrs. Patsy Cole came up to me and said, "God created you to be a woman".

Shortly thereafter, Pastor Dr. Ronnie W. Goines—who would later become my spiritual father 'Pops'—called me to the altar. Before he said anything about my appearance or the lifestyle I was living, he hugged me and said "Wow! You're a beautiful little girl." I'd dressed like a boy for so long I found it difficult to identify myself as the woman God created me to be. I also thought

I did a great job with hiding that little girl from the world.

I was offended when Mrs. Cole told me God created me to be a woman. My rude response indicated as much. Her words spoke with authority and love, however, and reminded me that I didn't *look* like the woman God created me. But, when Pastor Dr. Ronnie W. Goines called me "a beautiful little girl", it brought a sense of security knowing *someone* saw me as a little girl. He'd seen the little girl I tried so hard to hide with boy clothes. This was the little girl I was too frightened to let anybody see because I didn't know who to entrust her with.

The approach of these two Holy Spirit led individuals made it easier for me to respond to Jesus Christ when I had my first personal encounter with the Holy Spirit. Let's not forget that faith comes by hearing the Word of God and that the Word is Truth spoken in love (*Romans 10:17* and *Ephesians 4:14-15*). People need to hear Truth in order to believe it again.

Before that point in my life, all people I met wanted to be in grace with me. They never once said anything about my appearance or how the life I was living was wrong. To this day, the worst part of my story is not that I grew up without my biological father or that I was gay, abusive, on drugs, and completely out of my mind at times. The worst part of my story is that it took thirteen years for someone to approach me with Love and Truth.

I often ask myself where I would be if it weren't for them. If they'd chosen to remain silent or avoid me all together or simply just condemn me for how I looked, would I have known how to respond to God's conviction or to the Holy Spirit when I had my personal encounter with Him? If Mrs. Pasty Cole hadn't remind me that I was a woman or if Pastor Dr. Ronnie W. Goines would've ignored that little girl hiding behind boy clothes, I don't know where I'd be. What brothers me most is that, if it wasn't for them, I may have never seen *the way out*. Your approach sets individuals up to know how to respond when they have their personal encounter with the One who you should desire for them to surrender everything to: Jesus Christ.

The Wrong Approach Creates Defense Mechanisms

❖ A wise mentor once said "Jesus always meets us where we are because He understands what we've been through."

When a man comes to church dressed like a woman, or a woman comes to church dressed like a man, he or she is aware that they're going to a place where people have every right to call out sin. Yet, they still wake up and get dressed in the only clothes they may own to come to the house of the Lord seeking *the way out*.

On the way to church they've mentally exhausted all the scenarios in which they'll inevitably encounter immature Christians. These may include strange looks and loud whispers of those in disbelief that they'd come to church dressed like that. They become secretly embarrassed with nothing behind which to hide their sin. They fearfully anticipate someone to say something and prepare their defenses long before anyone has a chance.

Please note that gay identified individuals who come to your church are not always angry. They are mentally drained from all the judgmental snares, situations, and scenarios they know they'll face. It starts the moment they get out of the car, walk through the parking lot and enter the foyer.

By the time they make it to the sanctuary, they are mentally and emotionally beat.

In addition to that, a pastor, usher or other member of the congregation may say something like "Being gay is a sin", or confront them with "Why did you come to church like that?" Some people may even shift their attention from the sermon to focus on the gay person. Can we really be surprised when he or she responds defensively or stops going to church? When a person operating in homosexuality comes to your church, they prepare themselves for every condemnatory comment you can imagine. But, the one thing they don't prepare for is to be loved with God's kind of love.

Gay people's defensiveness is not always because they are gay. It could it be that they are subconsciously responding to the first person that rejected their same sex attraction when they initially "came out". If they come to your church, approach them with a hug, get to know their real name, and slowly gain their trust through relationship so that you can then ask those hard questions. Treat them like the first time guest that you soon want to join your church and get saved like you do with everyone else before you learn about their sin.

Sometimes, people force gay people out of a church by simply ignoring their presence. Others secretly pray they stop coming because they don't want to be known as 'the gay church'.

Others are homophobic. Their declaration that homosexuality is a sin is a license to openly express their anger and disgust towards those who practice it.

Galatians 6:1 admonishes us: "Brothers and sisters, if someone is caught in a sin, you who live by the Spirit should restore that person gently. But watch yourselves, or you also may be tempted." In this Scripture I don't think God is telling us to watch ourselves like their sin can be contagious but to be watchful of our own weaknesses that we're are not tempted in anyway in our approach to restore your brother or sister. Be watchful that your approach doesn't lead you to judge them or treat them harshly because their sin is different from the sin you overcame.

Discovering a Better Approach

❖ *Ephesians 4:14-15:* "…Instead, speaking the truth in love, we will grow to become in every respect the mature body of him who is the head, that is, Christ."

For the sake of this book, my assumption is that a majority of its readers fall into the category of a believer who finds it challenging to approach a person practicing homosexuality. By way of definition, the word 'challenge' means to invite competition. As Christians, we often overhear and become aware of the way in which a person battling with homosexuality can take offense when approached with Truth. So, could it be that homosexuality in and of itself is not a challenging topic? Could it be that we as believers have become so *intimidated* by a defensive response and fear of inciting them to riot that we feel defeated before we even make an attempt to approach them? Knowing this, many believers become timid instead of finding a more effective method of connecting with these individuals.

In part, the lack of communication is largely due to a history of not knowing the best way to communicate. The problem has thus become two fold. First, homosexuals live in constant mental fear of public correction. Second, they've experienced embarrassing judgmental situations. The church lives in fear of opposition and, as a result, says nothing *or* spews too much of the Word without the leading of the Holy Spirit.

As we know now, when using the Word, the body of Christ should take care to speak it in love. Word without love does not lead the person to Christ in a way that provides hope for healing. Do you think Jesus preached at the prostitutes and tax collectors He hung out with in a legalistic manner right after meeting them? They wouldn't have stuck around long enough to hear Him say anything else!

We must shine a light on the importance of examining our hearts and motives when we feel to approach someone operating in homosexuality. We must individually evaluate our desired outcomes. If the motive is simply to point out someone's sin because it's wrong and they shouldn't be living that way, you may need to re-examine your heart and refrain from saying anything at all. If there's no desire to love the person while showing them *the way out*, you're only leaving a person to deal with a constant feeling of condemnation that only leads to perpetuation of defeatism and further sin. We know this contradicts God's heart and ultimate desire for how He requires us to lead others to Him.

Romans 8:1 says "There is now no condemnation for those that are in Christ Jesus, because through Christ Jesus the law of the Spirit who gives life has set you free from the law of sin and death". We want to be careful not to condemn them to their actions. Instead, we want to offer the option of repentance by ushering them into a more intimate relationship with Christ. At the same time, we want to help them understand that "if we confess our sins, he is faithful and just and will forgive us our sins and purify us from all unrighteousness." (*1 John 1:9*).

A common misconception and the first line of defense that those struggling with homosexuality run to when feeling judged is 'God loves me' or 'God created me this way.' They hear 'homosexuality is a sin' or 'you're going to hell' so much that it makes it very difficult for them to hear any hope, let alone see *a way out*. Truth be told, most of the people telling them it's a sin can't help them see *the way out* either, which can leave a person feeling trapped. In this case, a proper response would be helping them understand that though nothing can separate them from God's love, their unbelief and way of living has created a breach in their relationship with Him (*Romans 8:31-39* and *Isaiah 59:2*).

Along with His love, God's ultimate desire is to see us made whole, free from sin, and restored into right relationship with Him. This may include an entire lifestyle change. Our goal should be inviting them into a relationship with Christ, not making them become a Christian out of the fear of hell. He who is wise wins souls (*Proverbs 11:30*). We must therefore use wisdom in our approach by helping a person recognize the position they've put themselves in spiritually by practicing homosexuality. We are to do this without ignoring the reality of their humanity.

What The Way Out *is* and *is Not*

- The real *way out* is to be born again by accepting Jesus Christ as one's Lord and Savior. This leads to a new life in Jesus Christ that is defined by what He says.

- The real *way out* provides power to live in holiness. We are set apart for God and no longer in bondage to sin.

- The *way out* is not changing exchanging sexual orientation from homosexuality to heterosexuality. This is a misguided initial focus. Through the real *way out*, however, anything is possible because God places His desires in the hearts of those who seek Him (*Psalm 37:4* and *Philippians 2:13*).

Romans 6:14-18: "For sin shall no longer be your master, because you are not under the law, but under grace. What then? Shall we sin because we are not under the law but under grace? By no means! Don't you know that when you offer yourselves to someone as obedient slaves, you are slaves of the one you obey—whether you are slaves to sin, which leads to death, or to obedience, which leads to righteousness? But thanks be to God that, though you used to be slaves to sin, you have come to obey from your heart the pattern of teaching that has now claimed your allegiance. You have been set free from sin and have become slaves to righteousness."

Key Points of the Way Out Process

- Helping those with unwanted same sex attraction (SSA) to obtain healing and redemption

- Offering a safe environment to be transparent

- Providing personal accountability and prayer partners

- Offering porn blocking software, i.e.: www.conventeyes.com, www.x3watch.com

- Providing exposure to healthy families

- Providing resources and education about SSA and the practice of homosexuality

- Assisting understanding of spiritual warfare

- Assisting understanding of process and the power of forgiveness

- Teaching sexual integrity

First Corinthians 10:13: "No temptation has overtaken you except what is common to mankind. And God is faithful: he will not let you be tempted beyond what you can bear. But when you are tempted, he will also provide the way out so that you can endure it."

All people struggling with homosexuality know their lifestyle is wrong and that being gay is a sin because God hasn't create anything He can't speak to. The Truth, however, has been suppressed by their iniquity. Scripture reminds us in *Romans 1:18-19* these individuals "…suppress the truth by their wickedness, since what may be known about God is plain to them because God has made it plain to them. For since the creation of the world God's invisible qualities—his eternal power and divine nature—have been clearly seen, being understood from what has been made, so that people are without excuse."

In light of this, everyone goes through a level of conviction prior to engaging in the practice of homosexuality. However, they may not necessarily know how to make sense of those convictions, let alone how to respond and find the way of escape. Therefore, we must not only be willing to show them *the way out*, but to actually walk it out with them. We want our approach to encourage them with the hope that God is faithful and that He won't allow them to be tempted beyond what they can bear.

This is the hope that assures them that, if and when they are tempted, He'll provide *the way out (1 Corinthians 10:13)*. We have to empower them to believe God can and will give them the ability to find the way of escape by overcoming their same sex desires or learning to endure. It is absolutely critical that we offer unbridled support to those seeking deliverance because the journey can be very challenging, confusing, and lonely.

Remember *Galatians 6:1*. It says "Brothers and sisters, if someone is caught in a sin, you who live by the Spirit should restore that person gently. But watch yourselves, or you also may be tempted. Carry each other's burdens, and in this way you will fulfill the law of Christ." In the forthcoming 'Salvation' heading, you will find tips to help you initiate the salvation process with those who are struggling with homosexuality and are seeking salvation.

Salvation

If a person struggling with homosexuality is not a believer, their sexual struggle is not your top priority. The objective then becomes seeing if they want to accept Jesus and thereby be saved. After this step, they are in a position to receive the words we have to give. This allows them to enter a safe place spiritually, enabling them to receive forgivingness and begin the healing process. This process simply involves them understanding and declaring *Romans 10:9*: "If you declare with your mouth, 'Jesus is Lord', and believe in your heart that God raised him from the dead, you will be saved."

Salvation is only the first step to these individuals' healing process. They, like every other believer, must then learn to walk out their deliverance. It's essential that they have a support or accountability system to assist their process of coming out of the lifestyle they've engulfed themselves in. It is important to partner with someone in the church to walk alongside them for the long-road to recovery.

Approach the person by asking 'Can I ask you a personal question?' Then, ask the following questions to initiate the salvation process.

- **Do you believe in Jesus Christ?**

- **Have you accepted Jesus Christ into your heart? Are you saved?**

- **Do you believe practicing homosexuality is against the will of God?**

You can't educate someone about the Word if they don't believe in the One who wrote it. So, these three questions are critical. If they answer 'no' to the second question, they have a much bigger issue than struggling with homosexuality. They need to be saved. We should never assume that all gay people believe in or know Jesus. Belief incites salvation, which is necessary to proceed on the *journey of the way out*. Also, we must be careful when holding them accountable to a standard of living they know nothing about. Therefore, you might have to introduce them to Him.

If they answer 'yes' to the first or second question, you've just made it easier for them to answer the third question without taking offense as easily. Though some may not understand why being gay is a sin, they've already acknowledged the only *way out* just by believing in God. Telling you they believe being gay is a sin is an *amazing* sign. It means they acknowledge Truth but haven't learned how to respond to their personal convictions about their behavior or don't know what the repentance process looks like.

Whether they respond 'yes' or 'no' to the third question, ask them if they've ever read what the Bible says about those who practice homosexuality. Then, grab one and show them, referencing some of the Scriptures discussed earlier in this Guide such as *Romans 1:18-32*. Once you begin walking with them toward *the way out*, you'll also show them their responsibility as a Christian and how to die daily to themselves with or without accountability (*Romans 12:1-2*). Our hope is that they begin to see the beauty in suffering for Christ despite their opposing desires. We hope they become able to sacrifice anything or any relationship blocking their path to *the way out*. This takes time so don't flood them with too much at once.

Sometimes, in their process of salvation and seeking change, most of their hope will be found in them not having same sex desires anymore or attractions. Some will base their growth off those two alone. Even though it is possible for God to completely remove same sex attractions, the fact is their homosexual desires or SSA *may* never go away even after salvation.

They should find encouragement in understanding *2 Corinthians 12:9*: "But he said to me, 'My grace is sufficient for you, for my power is made perfect in weakness.' Therefore, I will boast all the more gladly about my weaknesses, so that Christ's power may rest on me." They should also hold on to the promise of *Hebrews 2:17-18:*

"For this reason he had to be made like them, fully human in every way, in order that he might become a merciful and faithful high priest in service to God, and that he might make atonement for the sins of the people. Because he himself suffered when he was tempted, he is able to help those who are being tempted."

> ❖ A wise mentor once said "The very thing that we're asking God to remove could be that thing that keeps us closest to Him. In other words, our worst temptations could be responsible for keeping us on our knees seeking God."

Deliverance

It's important to make sure they understand deliverance doesn't start when they stop feeling or practicing homosexuality. It begins when they choose to take the time to make themselves available to God's Truth. God tells us the importance of surrender in shown in *2 Chronicles 7:14*. Only then can God commence the process of renewing their minds and purifying their hearts. Encourage them not to forsake the assembly of the saints, no matter how long their process takes.

Renewing the Mind

Most people battling with identity really don't know who they are outside of being gay. It is vital that they know. When a person is seeking *the way out*, they go through a process of God renewing their mind. They also have to learn how to not treat or see themselves as gay. This means that they must go back to the unknown. They all remember what that was like before they shared or acted on the emotion of same sex attraction. That fact by itself can start off as a very difficult process. This person can seem to have another sort of identity crisis as they are trying to navigate through who they were, who they are now and who God says they are.

Please know that this is a process can be very emotional and sometimes scary or depression for some, the will need a strong spiritual support system in place. Remember it's always much deeper then just being gay. That's just the result of the root but not the main issue. You may walk in just waiting to address their sexual issue and quickly find that's the least bit of their problem. Be prepared to shift in the direction their story pulls you in. To focus on the main problem, you must not just remove the bandage but open some well stitched wounds.

When someone opens the door to allow you to help them, don't be afraid to go in and out the door they opened. Don't be afraid to check on them and ask those hard questions, hold them accountable to what they said they wanted to do, or of saying something stupid. Guess what: You're human and you might say something or upset them when asking a simple question. But if you don't, the rejection that can grow between you two if you don't check can have a deeper negative effect. At least, when you say something they know you still love them and care even after everything they have told you. Rejection is big for a person in homosexuality so your silence and not checking on them can feel like rejection to some.

Obedience

Individuals on a journey out of the lifestyle must understand that we all have a personal responsibility as a Christian to seek growth. This is not applicable only to just babies in Christ or believers of many years. It is for everyone. Reading the Word is critical to their growth, renewing their mind and changing their perspective of how they feel about themselves, the world, church, and God. In *Matthew 16:24-26*, Jesus told his disciples, "If anyone would come after me, let him deny himself and take up his cross and follow me. For whoever would save his life will lose it but whoever loses his life for my sake will find it. For what will it profit a man if he gains the word and forfeits his soul? Or what shall a man give in return of his soul?"

The best way to explain this process to them is that God will enable them to carry all their sinful desires in their flesh without acting upon them until He takes the desires away or teaches them how to endure through the temptations. In other words, obedience is given life by walking in faith. Encourage them to get familiar what Paul speaks about in *2 Corinthians 12:8-10*. Remember *Proverbs 30:5:* "Every word of God is flawless; he is a shield to those who take refuge in him." Have them read *Proverbs 3* and memorize the well-known Verses five and six.

Literature and Scripture

Another tip is to encourage these individuals to read books written by others that have overcome similar things found in their stories and what they did to stay delivered. I've found this to be a great help. I suggest *Nothing Gay About Being Gay* as it will help take them on a journey of life wherein they will learn where their triggers started and how the enemy used these triggers to create strongholds in their life. This also is a tool to help these learn how to talk about their childhood and things that took place before coming out as gay.

First and foremost, however, it is important to provide them with Scriptural references or a Bible study plan for them to examine until the next meeting. This should help them gain an understanding of God's Word and the spiritual context of the battle they're fighting. It also creates opportunities for God to speak to them in their alone time, with which they may or may not have prior experience. *Romans* chapters *five* through *eight* consistently tell us what the gospel is, what Christ has done for us, and what you can expect of Him. *Romans* chapter *one* provides a glimpse of how God sees the spiritual influences of homosexuality in hopes that they receive revelation during their private time with God. I also suggest you encourage them to study the

Word preached on Sunday and during Bible study at their home church. They should consider doing this every week during their alone time to gain Biblical understanding in all areas and stay on one accord with the church.

As time progresses, allow them to talk through their personal interpretations of Scriptures they've studied as well as what they got concerning themselves after reading *Nothing Gay About Being Gay* or any other material that you offered or they found. Encourage them to identify their own triggers that led them on their same sex attractions. If they haven't already done so, support them in sharing their personal story. Create a safe space by sharing some of your own personal experiences and things that may have triggered you to act on certain things you knew were sinful before you chose to walk in obedience. I've listed discussion questions to consider below.

- **Where you ever mad at God because you felt He gave you this desire for the same gender and then said you weren't allowed to express it how you wanted to?**

- **When did you exchange the Truth you felt about your same sex desires for a lie?**

- **Who or what made it easy for you to believe being gay was okay?**

- **Do you remember the mental battle you went through before you openly expressed your same sex attraction? In other words, what was it like for you personally before you told anybody your secret?**

- **Did this battle make you question the nature of God or His unconditional love for you?**

- **How did the people who raised you react when they found out you were gay?**

When most people find out their loved one is gay, they react. The person that is expressing these feelings needs a compassionate response, not an emotional reaction. People who react emotionally can't see past the same sex attraction and people that respond have an understanding that same sex attraction is not the root issue.

When a person shares their same sex attraction for the first time, they are not seeking anybody's permission. Their mind is already made up. Now, they're on a mission to see how others will respond to their actions. When debating whether they should act on how they feel, they sometimes reason that they should just choose their emotions and give up on God completely. Now they are in search for answers—deeper answers! Most of their search for answers can be found in the responses of loved ones.

These questions will help you find the triggers that were used to deceive them even more into believing that they had to act out on the emotions. These questions can also be the introduction to the root of their burdens. Therefore, it is important to listen very closely. All gay people remember the times they exchanged the Truth about God for a lie. They remember the reasons they found to continue to hide the Truth they once acknowledged as Truth. I may not use those exact words. They all remember, however, those sleepless nights trying to make sense of something they felt wasn't right but also derived pleasure from.

For the person ministering, it is necessary to keep in mind that this is something they have also learned to suppress strongly. In the beginning, some may have no idea on how to express how they fell victim to the emotions. If you listen to their story, you can point out to them what you believe led them there. If you're wrong, they will correct you by informing you of what they believe led them there. Just listen!

How to Respond When Someone with Same Sex Attractions *is Not* Engaged in Same Sex Sexual Activity

> ❖ *Second Corinthians 10:5:* "We demolish arguments and every pretension that sets itself up against the knowledge of God, and we take captive every thought to make it obedient to Christ."

Explain to them that, if they start to practice a homosexual lifestyle, they open themselves up to a plethora of both spiritual and mental strongholds. More often than not, when people hear the words 'same sex attraction', they automatically equate that with being gay. However, same sex attraction alone does not mean a person is gay. It simply means they're being tempted to be gay. Being homosexual is not defined by the same sex attraction itself. Homosexuality truly occurs when someone chooses to embrace or act on their desires by engaging in relationships or sexual activity with someone of the same gender. If someone approaches you and shares that they are or have been attracted to the same gender and/or having same sex thoughts and desires, it does not mean they're gay or a homosexual but that they're being tempted to act out in this way. It doesn't mean they're gay or a homosexual.

How you should respond:

- **Respond to the humanistic need before addressing where they are spiritually. (i.e. hugging or consoling them if they're emotional)**

- **Commend them for trusting you with this information and being responsible enough to seek spiritual guidance before acting on their desires.**

- **Respond to their main concerns by helping them understand the ways in which they're being tempted to be gay, letting them know the enemy can only tempt us with things we are already attracted to—even if they don't know where the attraction came from. "But each person is tempted when they are dragged away by their own evil desire and enticed. Then, after desire has conceived, it gives birth to sin; and sin, when it is full-grown, gives birth to death." (*James 1:14-15*).**

- Show them how the enemy begins to entice our emotions depending on what and who we surrounded ourselves with.

- Ask them who they spend time with and what may be stimulating this emotion.

- Ask them if they are watching porn.

- Ask them how often they surround themselves with people who practice homosexuality and if these people ever encourage them to try living a gay lifestyle.

- Ask them to tell you about their childhood and listen without any interruptions.

- Explain to them how they are not gay, but merely being *tempted* to be gay, pointing out how some of the things they've mentioned could be potential triggers.

- Offer a deeper spiritual understanding; have them read *Romans 1:18-32* to further illustrate the consequences of not separating themselves from

whatever is enticing their personal temptations.

- **Finally, connect them with a trusted leader or ministry group for continuous support and accountability.**

We must change the notion and narrative that experiencing same sex attraction automatically equates to homosexuality. However, until they gain an understanding of the spirit they're battling, it's wise for them to separate themselves from anything or anyone enticing them to want to act on this desire. At this point, we're trying to prevent them from engaging in the practice of homosexuality. Therefore, helping someone understand their thoughts and feelings are merely a temptation and not who they are is very important. Until you can get to the root of what's triggering those thoughts and desires, continue to encourage them not to ponder or act on them or people that feel no conviction towards the practice of it.

How to Respond When Someone *is* Engaged in Same Sex Sexual Activity

Unlike just having same sex attractions, someone expressing that they're sexually active with an individual of the same gender means they are actively gay or engaged in the practice of homosexuality. The key to ministering to this person is to find ways to utilize the section called 'What The Bible Says About Homosexuality' on page 29. You must use compassion and love to help them understand the position they're putting themselves in spiritually and the other harmful things they could be exposing themselves to by engaging in homosexuality.

Below are responses you should use.

- **Respond to their humanistic need by either embracing or consoling them if they are emotional.**

- **Listen to them while staying composed. Do not overreact out of emotion.**

- **Invite them to discuss it further on a spiritual level.**

- If they're open to learning what God says about homosexuality, explain the breakdown of Scripture I referenced under the 'What Does the Bible Say About Homosexuality?' heading on page 29.

- Emphasize how much God loves them and doesn't take their step to ask for help lightly but that He honors that in a major way.

- Help them understand how to separate their selves from what they have been practicing.
- Ask them how long have they been feeling convicted about their lifestyle.

- Discuss what likely happened in the beginning stages of their temptations.

- Illustrate how they can be healed, set free, forgiven and explain that the relationship can be restored through repentance.

- Explore what motivated them to reach out.

Ask the following questions to get a better idea of what made them want to act on their desires.

- **Were you ever ashamed of the feeling you had when you first recognized it?**

- **How did you try to fix it in the beginning stages?**

- **Who extended the invitation for you to act on your same sex desires?**

- **What relationship allowed or taught you to express these emotions freely, either verbally or physically?**

- **What happen in that relationship? Did it end well? How did it change you?**

- **Who were you before you identified as being gay?**

- **What about your natural gender do you disagree with?**

These questions will show you that those struggling with homosexuality go through a process before acting on the thought. This will show you in turn that most were trying to find a reason to not to be gay. These questions also reveal how everyone battling homosexuality accept an invitation into the lifestyle, typically from someone asking or telling them they're gay.

The insecurities they thought a homosexual lifestyle would take away soon resurface when they realize this lifestyle offers everything except truth and love.

There are many dark things about living a homosexual lifestyle that don't come to light until after they've entered the lifestyle and, by that time, it's too late. So, they begin to adjust. Although their journey towards change has nothing to do with making them want to be in a relationship with the opposite sex, asking the hypothetical questions below has the potential to reveal a lot about how they view relationships and the insecurities they have within themselves. It may also reveal what they didn't witness regarding the opposite gender while growing up. Lastly, it may reveal they have a secret longing for a healthy heterosexual relationship but that they don't believe they will find it.

- **Ask the man what he would expect from a woman if he were to date her and if he has seen those morals consistently in women throughout his life.**

- **Ask the woman what morals she would want a man to have if she were to date him and if she has seen those morals consistently in men throughout her life.**

- **Ask the man what scares him about being with a woman.**

- **Ask the woman what scares her about being with a man.**

Although it can be tricky, you want to find a way to balance out the non-sexual relationships between both males and females in the church. Those who are struggling may need both. On one hand, they're learning about their God-ordained identity from the same gender and, on the other hand, their social needs are met by interacting with those they relate to the most. In some cases, the ones who they relate to the most are members of the opposite gender.

Things to Mention to Parents in the Church Who Have Discovered Their Child or Adolescent is Identifying as Gay

The right approach and response is very vital for a child or adolescent who is battling with homosexuality. Your main goal as a parent or youth leader is to prepare yourself to never compromise the Word of God and to never bash or abandon a child for going through spiritual warfare. Once that child decides to act on their desire and embrace a homosexual lifestyle, you must begin to prepare for what's ahead.

It is important to have an open line of communication. Please keep in mind that you have no control over their attractions. You can still help them, however, through their emotional stages. You never want the same sex desires part of their lives to be a 'don't ask, don't tell' subject. Instead, provide a safe place for them to express their emotions about their lives at home.

If your child ever 'comes out' to you the first words out of your mouth should be 'I love you so much. Thank you for trusting me with that information.' Your actions and facial expressions should match your tone or you might lose your child forever. What you push away the gay community is willing to embrace. Trust me. I know. After he or she says those words 'I'm gay', most parents are in so much shock that they may not be able to even fix their mouth to say anything. They will not be able to think about the appropriate thing to say or the proper response to have.

If you're reading this book, chances are you've already gone through this process and, in retrospect, you can tell that you probably had the wrong reply. If so, you need to apologize to your child. Or, perhaps you said the right thing but had no clue what to do afterwards. If they can muster up the words to say anything, most parents only reply by saying "I love you no matter what". Try to stay away from saying 'I love you no matter what.' I've learned this statement can sometimes be interpreted as acceptance for their lifestyle choice. Saying 'I love you so much. Thank you for trusting me with that information' leaves room to have open dialogue.

Here's some advice for the parent that finds themselves in a situation wherein the child feels comfortable enough to share their emotions with you and 'come out of the closet'. First, hug the child and ask them why they feel that way. Listen with no interruptions! As you listen, make sure you listen for those things they will mention that will give you insight on what triggered those emotions, whether it is trauma, choice, or exposure.

As you're still holding them in your arms, let them know that you *love* them and would like to hear more about the way they feel and how long have they been feeling that way. You don't want to react like this is a life or death situation but you have to keep in mind that what they just shared with you is very much a life or death situation.

If your child comes out the morning before school, if possible, try to take off and spend that day having fun with them. Engage in loving them and growing to understand what being gay means to them while making sure they understand you're a 'safe space' or person for them to speak to. School is a different territory for them and, most of the time, the attack of the enemy grows stronger outside the presence of the parent when children come out to them.

Try to spend that day, regardless of whether it's a school day or not, to reassure them that they can always come back to you if they need anybody to talk to. Then, ask them how they feel after telling you. Listen with no interruptions! Don't run and tell friends and family members. Instead, go into your prayer closet to obtain composure and spiritual guidance from our counselor Jesus Christ.

Discussion Questions

- Why do you think you're gay?

- When did you start feeling this way?

- Do you have gay friends?

- Do you want to embrace this lifestyle or do you want to learn *the way out*?

When you listen to the their answers to these questions, it will give you clear insight on what's enticing them, tormenting them, or harassing them. It may also point you in the direction of what their root causes could be. Please warn the parent that their child will also go through levels of changes in their emotions and personality as they navigate through this confusing time. The fact they've come out to them is one thing. The fact they've come out to their peers, especially to those that identify as gay or who simply approve of the gay lifestyle, is a totally different mental ball game that brings lots of attention, popularity, and excitement.

Things to Be Aware of and Look For in the Home After Your Child Comes Out

- They become distanced or isolate themselves from the family

- They become very secretive

- Their feelings about who they are may change everyday

- They refuse to talk about their same sex attraction or lifestyle

- They become hostile or disrespectful

- They become overly emotional or defensive

- Their grades drop and they become lackadaisical

- A suspicion they're orienting their life around identity

- Adult children may separate themselves from the family completely because they believe if you don't accept their lifestyle,

you're rejecting them as a person. Some may simply reject family because the insecurities and shame they feel internally become harder to bear when they're in the presence of family members who don't live the same life they're trying to live. Them separating from family could have nothing to do with how you treat them but a reflection of how they feel about themselves leaving room for them to develop a pattern of self-sabotaging.

They can become disrespectful to their peers at home and in school. For your child that might seem to be 'out' and enjoying the lifestyle with no changes in action or physicality, it may not be a traumatizing experience for them yet. But, the fact remains that they're being deceived and lacking Truth and real Love. Everything they're experiencing is still counterfeit. The lifestyle may offer them everything else but the real Love and Truth. That is where your role as a parent comes in. No matter how they respond—even if they choose not to receive—they need the consistency of your love and family support. There is no such thing as a person who practices homosexuality in honor of God. Don't let the perception of their smiles fool you.

A General Approach For Dealing With Sexually Confused Children

As people, we can't control other people's perception of life. This is especially true for children. If you have lived long enough, you have realized there's no such thing as the perfect church or family. Being the church, you can become the counselor to some of your members that have children with gender issues. You may find that the parent coming to you with these issues may be taking the blame for their child's actions, believing they played a part in their decision.

Although it's not their fault on how their child perceives life, I advise you to challenge them to look objectively into their family dynamics and see if they can find something that may be one of the pieces as an influential role. Again, remind them that they are not to blame for their child's gender issues. For a person that has never experienced same sex attraction, it can be very difficult to understand how another person got to this point in their lives or make sense of the inner turmoil they're going through even after accepting salvation.

They're more likely just as confused as you are, as they're trying to figure out who they are, what they feel, and how/why this happened to them. They're also asking themselves 'Why me?' They're dealing with all of this while simultaneous wrestling with the inner torment of having an unnatural attraction that feels very natural to them. It can be quite overwhelming. As the child navigates through understanding their sexuality and trying to make sense of their desires, an even bigger point of confusion would be to try making sense of the varying viewpoints between their faith and their feelings while not disappointing their parents.

On one hand, they'll be embraced by a community of people who identify with what they're feeling as being gay, finding freedom, love, and being their true selves, while on the other hand possibly feeling rejection by the Christian community and parents who view their struggle as bondage and sin. Regardless of what modern culture and society declares, as God's people, you must be willing to gain Biblical clarity and understanding for yourselves. This must happen in order to bring forth Truth, hope, and love to people struggling with homosexual issues. I will attempt to answer some of the most common questions and concerns you may have to address with the parents coming to you for help.

Ask the parent if they have ever had or prepared to have age appropriate conversations about homosexuality, same sex attraction, or sexual identity, *where* identity comes from within their children, when they were exposed to it, or asked them to share their emotions or personal struggle they have against homosexuality. The effect of first mention is very important. The parent must be confident approaching this topic boldly while having compassion for the inner pain their child may be suppressing or not be aware of. It will help the parent see that their child is choosing a homosexual lifestyle as a coping mechanism to bring solace to an empty place within or a Band Aid to try to conceal a much deeper-rooted issue. If that parent is homophobic, they may find it hard to get these answers in order to help their child.

The goal of the parent should be to pray for God to heal their child's deepest inner core so that they can gain complete wholeness in their emotions, identity, spirituality, sexuality, and relationships, while discovering Biblical Truth for themselves. My prayer is that, after reading this section, you will find yourself with more hope, encouragement, peace, and knowledge about how to handle this issue. If this already has or ever hits home, you'll have a lot more compassion for your child. Your approach should always be to help your child understand what they are going through not to force change or your opinion.

When a parent finds out that their child is gay, it's very common to experience a flood of emotions and negative opinions and thoughts of confusion. This is especially when you the parent feel as though you've done the best you could to ensure they've had a safe, loving home. Maybe you know that you haven't done your best as a parent and feel guilty for the lack of things you couldn't provide for your child. Maybe you have no clue how your role as a parent could have played any part in your child's homosexuality. Whatever the case is, rest assured that you are not alone!

Frequently Asked Questions From Parents

1. Did I miss the signs?

2. Did I fail as a parent?

3. What are good resources and bad ones? How can we tell the difference?

4. Do I also embrace their same sex partner?

5. Do I attend a gay wedding?

With all of these questions and the varying emotions that accompany after hearing your child identifies as gay, your most important concern should be as follows. 'If I'm this devastated, disgusted, angry, and hurt about my child then how mentally and emotionally devastated is my child, the one who is actually dealing with the feelings?' The main question for you as a parent should be 'How can I help them understand what they're going through even though I've never experienced it personally?'

As parents, we can become so devastated with news or thoughts of our children being gay that we may miss our child coming out to us as an actual cry for help. No matter how happy they may seem, there is always a cry for love, affirmation, attention, and acceptance. However, in the moment, we can become so blinded by our feelings of disappointment that we forget that we're not the one dealing with the desires and thoughts of same sex attractions.

Many parents make the mistake of allowing their emotional reactions to overtake a more loving embrace and appropriate response. If we're honest, many of us have no clue what the appropriate response should be. We're devastated because we don't understand what, why, and how my child ended up with same sex attraction. Your child is devastated because they're dealing with a real feeling that has tormented their core and maybe has been doing so for quite some time. It's the unknown that most parents are actually afraid of.

For most parents who are Christians, the only thing they understand about homosexuality is that it's a sin. For example, when a child comes to you and tells you that they lost their virginity you have a general understanding of what they had to do to lose their virginity. You know what to teach your child about sex and any possible outcomes or consequences that may come as a result. You also know what preventative measures to take and what boundaries to set to protect your child. When a child steals, lies, or even use drugs you understand what they did. You understand how to discipline your child and what morals to teach your child about these things to try ensure that it doesn't happen again.

When your child tells you that they're gay, however, you may go blank on all the rationale. You don't understand, you've never experienced it and, to be honest, you don't know what it is. You may only picture your son sucking on a penis or being penetrated by another man. You may only picture your daughter having oral sex with another women or being penetrated by a woman wearing a strap-on. Your mind tends to become trapped in solely visualizing the sexual aspect of being gay or on your reputation as the parent with the gay child. You don't tend to focus on the spiritual battle or internal turmoil the child is feeling.

Remember that every moment with your child does not have to be a 'gay moment'. Some moments just need to be moments with your child and not centered on your child's struggle or lifestyle choices. You also don't always have to ask them if they're still gay or consistently remind them of their salvation and hell. This could turn a child away. It's not that they don't love you or want to be around you. They're just tired that all you see in them is the fact that they're still battling homosexuality.

Every moment doesn't have to be a teachable moment. Every moment doesn't have to be a Bible thumping moment or a moment to remind your child that they are in sin. Learn to accept what you can't change about your child and still find ways to enjoy them no matter where they are in their process. Always be prepared, however, to give a godly response when asked question by them about homosexuality or gender identity or when they try to sneak their lifestyle into a conversation to get a response of approval from you.

Did I Really Miss the Signs?

Almost every family has at least one child or relative they can assume to be gay… With boys, it may be is that one boy everybody wonders about because they see he has more effeminate mannerisms or interests and tends to be more affectionate or sensitive than other boys. With girls, it may be the case she's a female athlete that likes to play basketball and wear oversized or baggy clothes and is not a big fan of showing her emotions or having a relationship with a boy like most girls dream about.

Oftentimes, we may think or even say the something like the following phrase to our family members. 'I wonder if they're going to be gay when they grow up?' Some family members may even begin to call this kid a tomboy, punk, or soft boy. Remember life and death is in the power of the tongue and we must be careful when using these terms to describe a child prematurely based on how they act when they are still learning about who they are.

All children are looking for something to affirm who they are. Depending on how that question is answered, this could make or break a child. We may wonder, however, if these may have been the indications, there are no precise definite sign to let you know that your child will end up gay. However, it is never too early to start talking to your child about how they feel, likes, dislikes, interests, crushes to get a sense of how they interpret love, relationships, non-sexual intimacy and identity.

Parents, seek spiritual discernment by asking God to reveal to you things that may be happening to you child that you may not be aware of. Also understand that your child may pull away from you not because they don't love you but, in some way, they assume you feel how they feel about themselves: ashamed. Some kids really hate the fact that they have this struggle and feel others could grow to hate them because they know they're gay.

Although we can't judge our child based on their likes and dislikes, with younger children especially, we should be attentive to their interests if their participation in certain activities is out of balance. Don't automatically assume your child is gay but instead take a greater interest and inquire about their reasoning for taking an interest in certain activities that we deem to more suitable for the opposite gender. Don't make like anything is wrong with a boy playing with a Ken doll or a girl playing with car trucks.

It's important to balance your child's exposure with both typical male and female kinds of activities. If you find them leaning more towards things that can lead them away from embracing their natural gender identity, watch for how they interact with other kids of the same and opposite gender.

Understanding your child's rationale, however, can assist you in detecting if the motive behind their interest is coming from any type of cross gender confusion. This can help balance your child's feminine or masculine identity, to make sure they explore other attributes about themselves. Girl athletes who like wearing baggy clothes, for example, need to learn how to be feminine and womanly and carry herself as such.

Additionally, boys who feel most comfortable in feminine environments need to learn how to be men, how to be masculine and strong, how to treat women, and how to express emotions in healthy, strong ways. Some fathers tell their son that boys don't cry and only girls do. A boy can receive that as a dislike or rejection of their identity. They may consequently think that they're a girl at heart and at times turn more towards adopting feminine traits.

Children enjoy being appreciated for the kinds of activities they enjoy. You want your child to know that they can be fully the gender they were created to be. You want them to enjoy whatever activity, colors, or sports they like if these do not define or skew their perception of their identity in any way. Don't feel bad as a parent. Unfortunately, no one has gay radar that lights up when a child is developing same sex attractions or is feeling confused about being a boy or girl.

Adopting a gay identity is a process of many stages. Before a child understands what's going on within them and how to act out on the emotions they feel, many of these stages have already taken place. Most children don't know how to express it until they find someone to share or express that emotion with. Know that the Bible never speaks of homosexuality as a person's identity, but rather condemns homosexual actions. You as a parent, you should become able to *distinguish* behavior from identity.

Did I Fail as a Parent?

❖ A wise mentor once said "You only fail as a parent when you compromise the Word of God to prove the love you have for your child so they can feel more comfortable in their sin."

No matter how wrong homosexuality is, it is real for your child. Sometimes, the best thing you can do as a parent is to learn what *not* to do. As parents, we seem to manage everything in the lives of our children except their spiritual growth and their interpretation of Scripture. Your house should be a constant reminder of Biblical Truth even when they grow up and move out. This means you must live by example and not preach 'Do as I say and not as I do'. In this manner, any lifestyle choice they make when they're grown has nothing to do with you or how they were raised. *If* and *when* your child tries to make you choose them over your beliefs, don't compromise in fear of losing them.

For example, if your child comes to you and says 'If you don't accept me and my lifestyle the way I want you to, then we can no longer have a relationship.' They can also say something like 'If you continue to tell me that I'm living in sin or if you choose not to attend my gay wedding, then I will never talk to you again.' They can also accuse you of not loving them because of the person they choose to have a relationship with. Don't allow the spirit that influences them to manipulate you. Nine times out of ten, your adult child is not the one with the issue about your faith. They've known about your faith but they may be getting pressure at home from their partner/gay peer(s). They may ask the following questions.

- **Why can't I ever go to your parent's house with you or why can't I meet your family?**

- **Do they know we are together?**

- **Do they know we are in love?**

- **Do they even know you are gay?**

Once your child answers their partner/gay peer(s) with 'My parent is a Christian', they will likely begin to tell your child how Christians shouldn't judge. They'll pose that they're a parent who can't possibly love them if they don't accept them, who they are, or who their partner is. Your child's partner/gay peer(s) will begin to take personal offense due to you not allowing them into your house and will encourage your child to turn against you.

If and *when* they get to that point where they're forcing you to choose, you have already lost them and the only way to get them back is by strict obedience, prayer, and you standing with Jesus alone if you have to. Love your child endlessly, but never compromise Scripture for the sake of having a relationship with them or as a way of proving the love you have for them. If they make you choose, choose Jesus.

Even as a parent, you have to know when to walk away. *1 Corinthians 5:3-5* states "For you are my part, even though I am not physically present, I am with you in spirit. As one who is present with you in this way, I have already passed judgment in the name of our Lord Jesus on the one who has been doing this. So when you are assembled and I am with you in spirit, and the power of our Lord Jesus is present, hand this man over to Satan for the destruction of the flesh, so that his spirit may be saved on the day of the Lord."

What Are Good Resources and Bad Resources and How Can We Tell the Difference?

Aside from the Bible, no one resource will have all the answers nor will they all have all of the right answers or revelations about homosexuality, so the Bible has to become your main resource. Make sure that any resource you choose outside the Bible such as books, documentaries, classes, etc. lines up appropriately with Scripture.

Anything that is contrary to the Word of God will not be an appropriate resource. Anything affirming homosexuality would not be a good resource. There are many churches embracing the lifestyle and altering Scripture to make it more acceptable. Avoid these resources. Any resource that goes against the Word of God is a bad resource. Any resource that agrees with the Word of God is a good one.

What If I Have Accepted My Child and Am Now Feeling Convicted Upon Becoming Educated on What Homosexuality Really is?

You'll want to apologize to your child and make them aware of your conviction and what you have learned. You'll want to let them know what you can and can't affirm from here on out. Ask them if they would like to know what you learned that changed your mind about their lifestyle. You can also suggest that they have a personal Bible study with you. If they want to know more beyond that, you can suggest they read *Nothing Gay About Being Gay* as well as *The Way Out*. The Bible transforms us and any other book can only inform us.

Parents: General Do's and Don'ts

Do's:

- Leave all lines of communication open even during their same sex relationships. You don't have to accept the lifestyle choice in order for you to comfort them after a bad breakup or even during an argument they have with another person. Find ways to comfort without condoning.

- Prepare them for the persecution they may face from their peers or other Christians who mishandle the Word to only condemn them to their actions and not restore them to wholeness. Prepare them to know not to accept disrespect from anybody, in spite of their current choices.

- Make it a house rule for them not to attend any school groups about LGBTQ+ offered at school or join any outside gay functions while still under your roof.

- Make them feel comfortable enough to talk to you about anything, without judgment.

- Give your child room and space to figure things out on their own. Do this once you have established household boundaries.

- Be responsible with the secrets they share with you. Continue to affirm your child's born gender, no matter how they feel about themselves.

- If you have a child who was born intersex, teach them as early as possible about the potential entanglement of their emotions. Also teach them about any surgeries they had as a newborn to remove parts that developed during the process. Teach them to tell you if they ever start feeling confused about their gender and wondering if they should have been the opposite gender because of the birth defect.

- Learn the terms and symbols people use that identify the gay lifestyle.

<u>Don'ts:</u>

- Do not allow them to wear opposite sex clothing or purchase opposite sex clothing for them to encourage their preferred or chosen gender.

- Do not make a mockery of their same sex attraction. Do not make small jokes, neglect their natural being, or spreading the word around family.

- Do not make everything about their homosexuality.

- Do not overlook the seriousness of your child's struggle by calling it just a phase.

- Do not 'Bible-bash' your child by giving them Scriptures against same sex relationships every time, or nearly every time, you see them.

- Do not allow your child to put up gay pride paraphernalia in their room or in the home.

- Do not try to fix your children but educate them with love instead.

- Do not reject or dismiss how they feel about the same sex.

- Do not encourage them to date the same sex or force them to date the opposite sex.

- Do not allow your child to isolate themselves from family because of their struggle.

- Do not kick your child out of the house because of their same sex attraction.

- Do not try to scare them into a relationship with God by constantly telling them they will go to hell.

- Do not give everybody permission to approach your child about their same sex attraction in the attempt to try and save their soul without permission of your child.

- Do not make it seem like every time they get in trouble or do something wrong it's because they are trying to be gay.

- Do not compromise your belief to prove your love for a child or member of the church.

- Do not punish them for having same sex attraction. But, place the same boundaries you would if your child disobeys you by talking or doing things with the opposite gender you don't approve of.

- Do not expose them to the gay lifestyle of friends or family members until they're old enough to understand the demonic influence behind their gay friends or family members' actions.

- Do not allow a boy to dress how he feels, if it is outside the boundaries of his natural gender.

- Do not allow a girl to dress how she feels, if it is outside the boundaries of her natural gender.

- Do not allow unsupervised or unmonitored same sex sleepovers. These must be strongly monitored or out of the picture if you sense your child has this struggle. Now all friends are potential mates. Many people in homosexuality can share stories of how their first same sex sexual encounter was in their parents' house because they thought they were just friends. Sometimes, homosexual attraction blooms within friendships.

Do I Attend the Gay Wedding of My Loved One?

What you should ask yourself is 'What part of me attending a gay wedding will glorify God?' and 'What message will my attendance send to the same sex couple that's making a vow to publicly make a mockery of God till death till they part?' Remember the part of vows that state 'for better or for worse'. They've not only invited you to be a witness to their union. They will expect you to support them in all situations, as long as they live. Ultimately, you will not have God's peace.

First Corinthians 10:23 supports this by stating "I have the right to do anything, you say. Not everything, however, is beneficial. I have the right to do anything but not everything is constructive." Be mindful of the message you send by doing this. You don't want your witness to be spoken evil of. *Romans 14:16* reminds us "Therefore do not let what you know is good be spoken of as evil." Furthermore, *Genesis 2:21-25* says "Then the Lord God made a woman from the rib he had taken out of the man, and he brought her to the man. The man said, "This is now bone of my bones and flesh of my flesh she shall be called 'woman,' for she was taken out of man." That is why a man leaves his father and mother and is united to his wife, and they become one flesh. Adam and his wife were both naked, and they felt no shame."

How to Treat the Partner of My Child or Loved One

Treat him or her like a human being. You never have to refer to them as a couple. It can be tricky because you will find yourself attending events where they are both present, being that they're a couple. By you attending and supporting a birthday or graduation doesn't mean you approve of a lifestyle choice. There is a very thin line on how you express yourself at these functions because you are in their world. Be mindful. Your relationship with your friend, child, or loved one in the lifestyle needs to be just that.

Never attempt to disrespect their partner to show how much you disapprove of their life choice to prove you're a Christian. Everyone already knows that you are a Christian and is expecting you to act a certain way. Your loved one practicing homosexuality only needs to understand where *you* draw the line when it comes to events, celebrations, or functions you initiate.

Always be mindful of the setting you're in because you can become accepting of the romantic phrases, comments, and gestures the same sex couple pays back and froth. Sometimes, you can fall into believing their relationship seems to be healthier than some you have seen—even your own. You may in fact forget you're looking at sin at its best. The people experiencing the same sex desires are not bad people. The practice of homosexuality is, on the other hand, very deceiving. Each person has learned a skill to act a certain way to manipulate you into approval. Be watchful and alert.

Understanding Why People Go Back Into the Homosexual Lifestyle After Years of Being on the Straight and Narrow

❖ *James 1:18*: "Such a person is double-minded and unstable in all his ways."

A person's return to the lifestyle is not an indication of 'once gay, always gay'. There are specific situations that occur. In general they are typically watching porn all the time or masturbating a lot. They are having anonymous same sex sexual and non-sexual encounters secretly and they're not confessing their sins any longer to you or anyone else. This goes on for a long time without them reaching out for help consistently and, over time, they can become very heavy from continually being in a bad state of mind by living one way at church and one way outside of church.

When this happens to a person we call it back sliding but fail to think about the fact that, by the time someone goes back into the gay lifestyle, they've reached a period in their relationship with Christ where they have plateaued. They carry so much guilt they have ended the mental process of striving not to sin or thinking about what sin is. They have stopped thinking about what Jesus did for them to make them want to change in the first place. And, many times, they have conceived a new Jesus that does not line up with Scripture but simply based of how they feel.

These individuals label themselves as 'Type A' and 'Type B' homosexuals. Type A homosexuals are gay-affirming Christians. They believe in gay marriage and that they're fulfilling God's design towards their sexuality via homosexual practice. Type B homosexuals identify as gay Christians even though they practice celibacy and believe in the practice of monogamy. As we learned earlier in the Guide, having same sex attraction and participating in homosexual practice are two different things. Type A and Type B identified homosexuals haven't learned how to differentiate between the two.

Being gay is not against any worldly laws. That leaves most of us completely unaware of what the gay identity does to a person. They completely lose their bearings and end up going back into the gay lifestyle. It does not mean that it is normal or okay, even if they have some resemblance of spirituality. If you were to dive deeper and ask some probing questions, you will see this person has been in a bad place for a very long time and is misinterpreting a lot of things. Most of their choices are based off the sexual emotions they still feel toward the same sex after not gaining that same desire for the opposite sex. This can push a person back into homosexual practice so they can feed their need for emotional intimacy.

As a Christian, consider that when someone goes back to the lifestyle it didn't happen overnight. Normally they have company in their life that isn't a good influence on them. This company is likely a stronger influence than even they can admit to. We need to pray for these individuals fervently. We don't need to display attitudes like 'Well, I knew they would…' One of the ways you can tell someone is lost is that their life is very compartmentalized. They know of God but lack discipline.

Being gay is a hard temptation to defeat. A person must give almost everything to God so they can find balance. They cannot afford to be lukewarm in God. If they are lukewarm, their life will turn into an unhealthy tug of war. They must find stability. Unfortunately, this is something you can't give them. All you can do is pray and remind them of *the way out* process all over again.

You must accurately discern when to hand them over to the enemy. *1 Corinthians 5:3-5* states "For my part, even though I am not physically present, I am with you in spirit. As one who is present with you in this way, I have already passed judgment in the name of our Lord Jesus on the one who has been doing this. So, when you are assembled and I am with you in spirit, and the power of our Lord Jesus is present, hand this man over to Satan for the destruction of the flesh, so that his spirit may be saved on the day of the Lord."

The Way Out Conclusion

Keys for those seeking *the way out*:

1. Understanding the origins of your attraction (your past, the things that happened to you, how certain hurts entered, and facing the reality of certain disappointments). Facing certain hurtful moments including shameful moments that didn't make you feel accepted as a male or female and that left emotional scars and hurts. Also, how these scars are now being covered by homosexual activity. Acknowledging that homosexuality is an attempt to repair the unspoken hurt.

2. Stay honest with your own self. Think: 'If homosexuality is not a legitimate expression of human sexuality, then it must represent something else. And, that something else is my attempt to repair.' Don't give in to a false self because you want to keep people or yourself happy. You must stop living in an interactive way. Stay alive to your true self.

3. It is important to develop platonic same sex relationships to get your emotional needs met in a non-sexual way. Attention,

affection, and approval are vital. These are the emotional elements behind sex. You dent your personal inclination to isolate, to go into a self-protecting mode. Reach out to people. Be vulnerable. Experience new things. Then, you will discover your desire to act out on same sex attractions will be easier to endure or will fade away entirely.

4. Take responsibility for your behavior not from a Biblical, ethical, or spiritual sense but in a psychological sense. If you act out, what happened before you acted out? When someone admits they have backslidden, your first question should be 'What happened before you backslid?' Most will say 'I don't know' or 'I don't remember'. Give them a minute to think and they will share some incident of hurt or disappointment. Somebody did something or said something that triggered a past hurt. When hurt comes back, they choose homosexual practice. Out of habit, that's their default method of coping.

5. You have to develop a personal relationship with the Word of God. The Bible doesn't just tell you what to do but it gives you the strength to do what it is you need to do. Renewing of the mind, having a different perspective on what happened to you, and

what's now happening to you, is vital. Don't forsake the assembly of the saints. Find a good church home and go consistently. Find a place to serve behind the scenes like vacuuming the sanctuary, putting up chairs, cleaning, becoming a greeter, or joining a small group. This will keep you involved and an active part of the church.

6. For someone trying to overcome their same sex attraction, they must come to understand their personal triggers. It's important for you to learn your individual triggers and pay close attention to events that could initiate or even instigate the desire (i.e.: a recent argument with a loved one, work stress etc.).

7. You must confront the elements that led you into the lifestyle by practicing forgiveness. You must learn to develop healthy, non-sexual interactions with men and women.

8. It is a healthy for you to allow someone to teach you how to carry yourself as woman or a man according to their God-given gender. This includes but is not limited to how to sit, stand, or walk and to be intentional about reflecting their biological

sex. In conclusion, changing clothes means nothing without a changed mindset. For some, becoming the woman or man God created them to be will require a committed believer actively showing them appropriate masculine or feminine behaviors, while standing alongside them as a guide to help walk out the process. This may require breaking habits of pretend and digging deep to tap into their true selves.

I have attempted to address the most common scenarios in this Guide. While writing, I had to accept that it is impossible to address every possible scenario that I have personally experienced or heard of that has been effective in helping someone find *the way out* of and stay out of homosexuality. The Holy Spirit leads each person and every situation depending on His purpose for them. I do believe I successfully emphasized the most common scenarios so that you to understand what homosexuality really is and not what the world has made it out to be. If I didn't teach or touch upon questions relative to your own specific circumstances, please pardon me.

I didn't address some scenarios. These include how to open conversation with a child who is attending church with his gay parents and how to prepare a child who has a parent that comes out the closet. This parent could begin to identify as transgender and cross dress or introduce the child to their new partner after becoming divorced from the child's other biological parent. I trust that, through your own studies and the guidance of the Holy Spirit, you will be able to rightly navigate and come to peace with any scenario that presents itself. I would like to direct you to the Word in *2 Timothy 2:15:* "Do your best to present yourself to God as one approved, a worker who does not need to be ashamed and who correctly handles the word of truth." Go and learn what this means.

In *Matthew 9:13*, Jesus told His listeners to do their own Bible study. So, I encourage you to allow the Holy Spirit to guide you into all Truth. Thank you for reading. Take what you learned in this book into your personal prayer closet and have faith that God will help you uncover the specific answers you need for your own unique circumstances. This book is limited but the Holy Spirit is not.

I pray ***The Way Out*** has provided you with the hope and encouragement for you to be spiritually motivated and not emotional driven when it comes to showing someone the way out of any lifestyle of sin. I encourage you to move when God says move, speak when He says speak, love and be quiet when the Holy Spirit whispers 'Shhhh…' Remember that no matter how unequipped you feel, God will never contradict His Word or compromise his purpose based off the feelings of others. Let the Holy Spirit be your teacher, guide, and confidence.

I leave you with *Matthew 28:19-20*: "Therefore go and make disciples of all nations, baptizing them in the name of the Father and of the Son and of the Holy Spirit, and teaching them to obey everything I have commanded you. And surely I am with you always, to the very end of the age." There is only one *way out* and that *way* is you pointing every person to Jesus Christ. Thank you for reading.

Please visit www.tyeeshaholt.com for more material about identity and homosexuality. Tyeesha Holt Ministries is a developing ministry that appreciates all your support.

Made in the USA
Columbia, SC
02 April 2024